Introduction

to

Zi Wei Dou Shu – Si Hua Lineage

(四化紫微斗数)

Calvin Yap

Some of the information from this book was obtained from the Internet. Acknowledgement is given to the authors and/or creator of Wikipedia, Astro-databank and google in general. Any omission of acknowledgement is unintentional. Please inform the author so that such acknowledgement can be included in the next edition. All other intellectual property rights contained or in relation to this book belongs to Calvin Yap.

The authors can be reached at:

Email: Calvin Yap (calvin_yap@yahoo.com)

Website: http://www.fengshui-hacks.com/

Edited by: Denise Yap

Warning and Disclaimer

The information in this book is based on the author's knowledge and personal experience. It is presented for educational purposes to assist the reader in expanding his or her knowledge on Chinese Meta-physics. The techniques and practices are not to be used without any proper training. The author is not responsible in any manner whatsoever for any loses or damages caused or alleged to be caused directly or indirectly from using the information contained in this book.

The author provides onsite courses for those who are keen to learn. Please contact the author for arrangement.

Dedication and Acknowledgement

For my family:

> To my wife Lucy & my 2 daughters: Denise & Sherry for their understanding and support.

To Master Kang:

> For his unreserved sharing of Zi Wei knowledge.

Contents

Author's Note

My journey in learning Zi Wei Dou Shu started as an accident. Zi Wei Dou Shu has been under my radar for longest time but I did not manage to learn it for various reasons until my friend and celebrity chef, Daniel Tay suggested that I go over to Malaysia to learn from Master Jessmond Ong and Master Ng. It was an eye opening experience for me.

From there I bought an English book by Master Ng titled *Flying Star Zi Wei Dou Shu*. In that book, there is a foreword written by Si Hua Grandmaster, Kang Hui Huat. After some searching, I realised that Grandmaster Kang is from Singapore, and I managed to contact him. After meeting Grandmaster Kang, I decided to take private classes with him and subsequently completed his version of Si Hua Zi Wei Dou Shu.

Zi Wei Dou Shu is a very complex system for destiny analysis but it has a high level of accuracy. It gives you multiple dimensions of analysis. I hope this book will give you some insights into Zi Wei Dou Shu. However, to actually learn and understand how to analyse Zi Wei Dou Shu, I would suggest that you attend a proper course.

Lastly, the Zi Wei Dou Shu stars in this book are arranged by Palaces for easy reference.

Calvin Yap

Calvin_yap@yahoo.com
http://www.fengshui-hacks.com

Other books from Author:

1. Control Your Destiny by Mastering Qi Men Dun Jia (ISBN: 978-981-08-7136-9) (Out of print)
2. Qi Men Dun Jia (奇门遁甲) Chāi Bù (拆布) English Calendar 2011 – 2020 (ISBN: 978-981-08-7386-8)
3. Practical Application of Qi Men Dun Jia (ISBN: 978-981-08-9837-3)
4. Qi Men Dun Jia Compendium Series Volume 1 - English Chai Bu & Zhi Run Calendar 1930 – 2020 (ISBN: 978-981-07-0509-1)
5. Qi Men Dun Jia Compendium Series Volume 1 - English Chai Bu & Zhi Run Calendar 2020 – 2040 (ISBN: 979-868-82-1636-3)
6. Qi Men Dun Jia Compendium Series Volume 2 - 540 Yang Dun Chart (ISBN: 978-981-07-0510-7)
7. Qi Men Dun Jia Compendium Series Volume 3 - 540 Yin Dun Chart (ISBN: 978-981-07-0511-4)
8. FengShui at Your Fingertips (ISBN: 978-981-07-1670-7)
9. FengShui at Your Fingertips 2nd Edition (ISBN: 978-981-14-8731-6)
10. Controla Mejor Tu Destino Dominando Qi Men Dun Jia: Qi Men Dun Jia (Spanish Edition) (ISBN: 978-981-11-1618-6)
11. Le FengShui sur le bout des doigts (French Edition) (ISBN : 978-981-11-0436-7)
12. Better Control of Your Destiny by Mastering Qi Men Dun Jia (ISBN: 978-981-09-2079-1)
13. Fundamentals of Chinese Meta-Physics (ISBN: 978-981-11-3809-6)
14. Qi Men Dun Jia Made Easy (ISBN: 978-981-14-1107-6)

Translation by Author:

1. Basic Qi Men Dun Jia - How to become a Fengshui Master by Master Ye (ISBN: 978-981-07-1745-2)
2. Destiny Analysis Using Qi Men Dun Jia by Master Ye (not available to public)
3. Date Selection Using Qi Men Dun Jia by Master Ye(not available to public)

History of Zi Wei Dou Shu (紫薇斗数)

In most of the Zi Wei Dou Shu books available, it was said that Zi Wei Dou Shu was created by a Taoist named Lu Chun Yang (呂純陽) during the Tang Dynasty. Lu Chun Yang (呂純陽) is also known as Lü Dongbin (呂洞賓), the de-factor leader of the 8 immortals (八仙). In some books, it was mentioned that it was created by Chen Tuan (陳摶), another Taoist sage. It was said that Chen Xi Yi (陳希夷) later further developed it during the Song Dynasty and later on by Luo Hong Xian (羅洪先) during the Ming Dynasty to its present-day form.

However, according to Ho Peng Yoke in his book, ***Chinese Mathematical Astrology Reaching out to the stars***, he mentioned that modern Zi Wei Dou Shu came from Taiyi Rendao Mingfa method (太乙人道命法) with influence from Iranian, Hellenistic and Babylonian Astrology. From his research, it stated that the Zi Wei Dou Shu 12 palaces were derived from the Taiyi method. In addition, the 16 deities (十六神) in Taiyi are identical to the 16 stars used in Zi Wei Dou Shu.

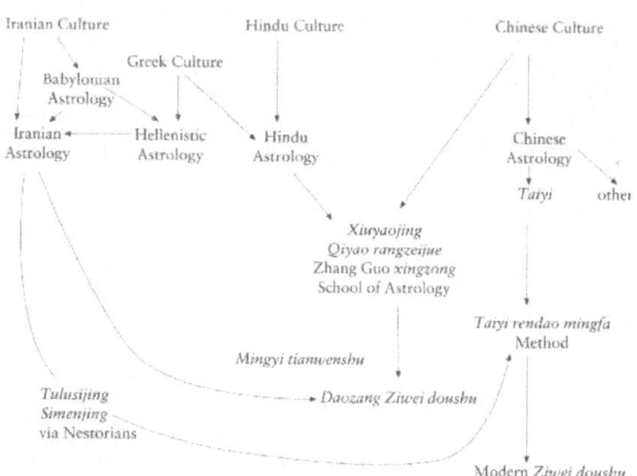

Figure 3.22 Transmission of the *Ziwei doushu* system of astrology.

Ho Peng Yoke: ***Chinese Mathematical Astrology Reaching out to the stars***

Lineage in Zi Wei Dou Shu

There are two lineages in Zi Wei Dou Shu. There is the San He lineage, and the Si Hua lineage.

The San He lineage is also known as the San He Triangle Harmony Lineage , and it uses 30 – 200 stars attributes. The chart is read by evaluating the Triangle Harmony of the 12 palaces and the attributes of the stars in these palaces. The San He lineage is also known as the Southern School of Zi Wei Dou Shu.

The Si Hua lineage is also known as the Flying Star lineage. This is based on the Si Hua formula or stars, in which, depending on the Heavenly Stem, the star is flown from one palace to other. It utilizes 14 main stars and 4 auxiliary stars (a total of 18 stars). The Si Hua lineage is also known as Northern School of Zi Wei Dou Shu.

It was said that the San He lineage of Zi Wei Dou Shu was stolen from the imperial palace. The emperor had falsified both the San He and Si Hua Zi Wei Dou Shu and released it to the public. The true copy of Si Hua Zi Wei Dou Shu was release only after the fall of Qing Dynasty.

Part I – Basic

Here are some basics that you would need to know before learning Zi Wei Dou Shu.

Basic

Five Elements

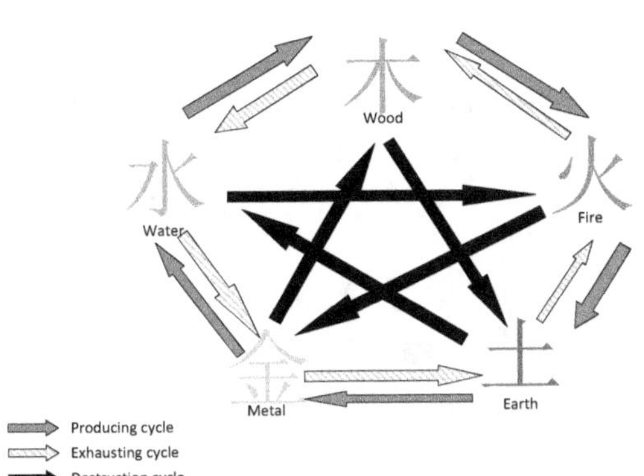

The concept of the Five Elements (五行) is the most basic fundamental as well as the most important concept to understanding the basic art of Chinese meta-physics. The Ancient Chinese Sage derived that the universe consists of five building blocks of elements; i.e. Earth, Metal, Water, Wood and Fire. Each element has its own attributes and characteristics. These five elements follow the law of nature as described below:

- Wood produces Fire, exhausts Water and controls Earth.
- Fire produces Earth, exhausts Wood and controls Metal.
- Earth produces Metal, exhausts Fire and controls Water.
- Metal produces Water, exhausts Earth and controls Wood.
- Water produces Wood, exhausts Metal and controls Fire.

He Tu (River Map)

It was said that the He Tu or River Map was derived from a mystical creature that emerged from the Yellow River – hence it is called River Map. On the back of this creature were black and white dots which formed a pattern.

	South Fire			
		7		
East Wood		2		West Metal
8	3	5, 10	4	9
		1		
		6		
	North Water			

The He Tu describes that 1 & 6 are North and the Water element. It can be described that a combination of 1 & 6 becomes Water. The same applies for 2 & 7, which is the Fire element and the resulting combination is also Fire.

3 & 8 or combination of both is the Wood element. 4 & 9 or combination of both is the Metal element. Finally, 5 & 10 combines to become the Earth element.

Luo Shu (Magic Squares)

According to the legend, it was said that a giant tortoise emerged from the river. Inscribed on its back were circular dots in 3x3 grid pattern. It is also known as Magic Squares.

	SE	South	SW	
East	4 Wood	9 Fire	2 Earth	West
	3 Wood	5 Earth	7 Metal	
	8 Earth	1 Water	6 Metal	
	NE	North	NW	

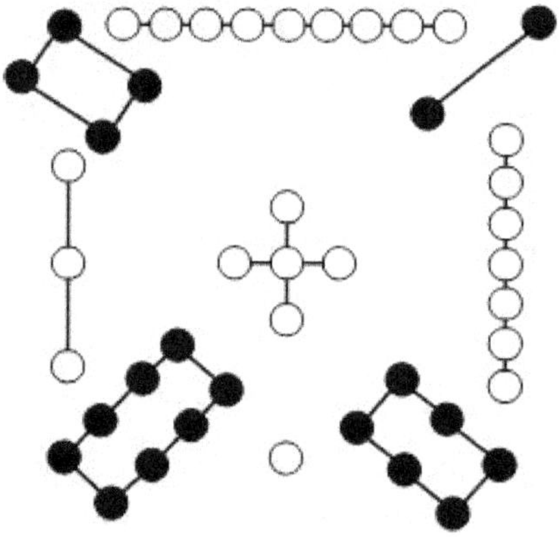

Ba Gua (Trigram)

It was claimed that Fu Xi was the person who invented the Ba Gua. There are 2 types of Ba Gua; Pre-Heaven and Post-Heaven. The tips to memorize the Ba Gua is as follows:

Ba Gua	Symbol	Memorizing (in Chinese)	Translation
乾 qián (Father)	☰	乾 qián 三 sān 连 lián	Qián is 3 links
兌 duì (Youngest Daughter)	☱	兌 duì 上 shàng 缺 quē	Duì lack the top

離 lí (Middle Daughter)	☲	離 lí 中 zhōng 虛 xū	Lí middle void
震 zhèn (Eldest Son)	☳	震 zhèn 仰 yǎng 盂 yú	Zhèn is an upward-facing jar
巽 xùn (Eldest Daughter)	☴	巽 xùn 下 xià 斷 duàn	Xùn is broken off at the bottom
坎 kǎn (Middle Son)	☵	坎 kǎn 中 zhōng 滿 mǎn	Kǎn is full in the middle
艮 gèn (Youngest Son)	☶	艮 gèn 覆 fù 碗 wǎn	Gèn is an upside down bowl
坤 kūn (Mother)	☷	坤 kūn 六 liù 斷 duàn	Kūn is 6 broken lines

In Chinese Meta-physics, the Post-Heaven Ba Gua is mostly used. The Pre-Heaven Ba Gua is only used to supplement any formula if needed.

The lines are derived from the Taiji where the Chinese believe that the universe is made of positive and negative energy balancing each other. When there is sunlight, there will be darkness; when there is strength, there will be weakness.

The Taiji shows that everything is in a virtuous cycle with the blending of Yin and Yang influences. This is the inter-locking of black and white as shown in the Taiji symbol. The stronger (white) element is denoted as Yang, and the weaker (black) element is denoted as Ying. Therefore, sunlight is Yang whereas darkness is Yin. Movement is Yang and stationary is Yin. Therefore, in Feng Shui, a mountain is considered as Yin, while water is considered as Yang. In a natural environment, water collects in mountain and forms river.

In Taiji you will notice that within Yin there is Yang and within Yang there is Yin. Looking at the Taiji chart, you will find that within the black there is white and within the white there is black. This means that within light there is darkness, and within darkness, there is light. The Taiji is further derived into solid and broken lines. The solid line denotes Yang or Male and the broken line denotes Yin or Female.

This is a Yang line and it denotes Male. This is a Yin line and it denotes Female. Then the solid line and broken line are further arranged to form the Ba Gua.

The Pre-Heaven Ba Gua layout on 3 X 3 grids is as follows:

兌 duì Youngest Daughter Metal, 4 Lake	乾 qián Father Metal, 9 Heaven	巽 xùn Eldest Daughter Wood, 2 Wind
離 lí Middle Daughter Fire, 3 Fire	5	坎 kǎn Middle Son Water, 7 Water
震 zhèn Eldest Son Wood, 8 Thunder	坤 kūn Mother Earth, 1 Earth	艮 gèn Youngest Son Earth, 6 Mountain

The Post-Heaven Ba Gua layout on 3 X 3 grids is as follows:

巽 xùn Eldest Daughter Wood, 4 Wind	離 lí Middle Daughter Fire, 9 Fire	坤 kūn Mother Earth, 2 Earth
震 zhèn Eldest Son Wood, 3 Thunder	5	兌 duì Youngest Daughter Metal, 7 Lake
艮 gèn Youngest Son Earth, 8 Mountain	坎 kǎn Middle Son Water, 1 Water	乾 qián Father Metal, 6 Heaven

Ten Heavenly Stems

The attributes of Ten Heavenly Stems is as follows:

Heavenly Stems	Attribute
Jia (甲)	Yang Wood
Yi (乙)	Yin Wood
Bing (丙)	Yang Fire
Ding (丁)	Yin Fire
Wu/ Ji (戊 / 己)	Yang Earth / Yin Earth
Geng (庚)	Yang Metal
Xin (辛)	Yin Metal
Ren (壬)	Yang Water
Gui (癸)	Yin Water

Twelve Earthly Branches

The attributes of twelve earthly branches is as follows:

Earthly Branches	Element	Animal	Time	Season
子(Zi)	Yang Water	Rat	23:00 – 00:59	Winter
丑(Chou)	Yin Earth	Ox	01:00 – 02:59	Winter
寅(Yin)	Yang Wood	Tiger	03:00 – 04:59	Spring
卯(Mao)	Yin Wood	Rabbit	05:00 – 06:59	Spring
辰(Chen)	Yang Earth	Dragon	07:00 – 08:59	Spring
巳(Si)	Yin Fire	Snake	09:00 – 10:59	Fire
午(Wu)	Yang Fire	Horse	11:00 – 12:59	Fire
未(Wei)	Yin Earth	Goat	13:00 – 14:59	Fire
申(Shen)	Yang Metal	Monkey	15:00 – 16:59	Autumn
酉(You)	Yin Metal	Rooster	17:00 – 18:59	Autumn
戌(Xu)	Yang Earth	Dog	19:00 – 20:59	Autumn
亥(Hai)	Yin Water	Pig	21:00 – 22:59	Winter

Twelve Earthly Branches Three Harmony Combination

- Yin- Wu - Xu combination as Fire frame.
- Si –You - Chou combination as Metal frame.
- Shen – Zi - Chen combination as Water frame.
- Hai- Mao - Wei combination as Wood frame.

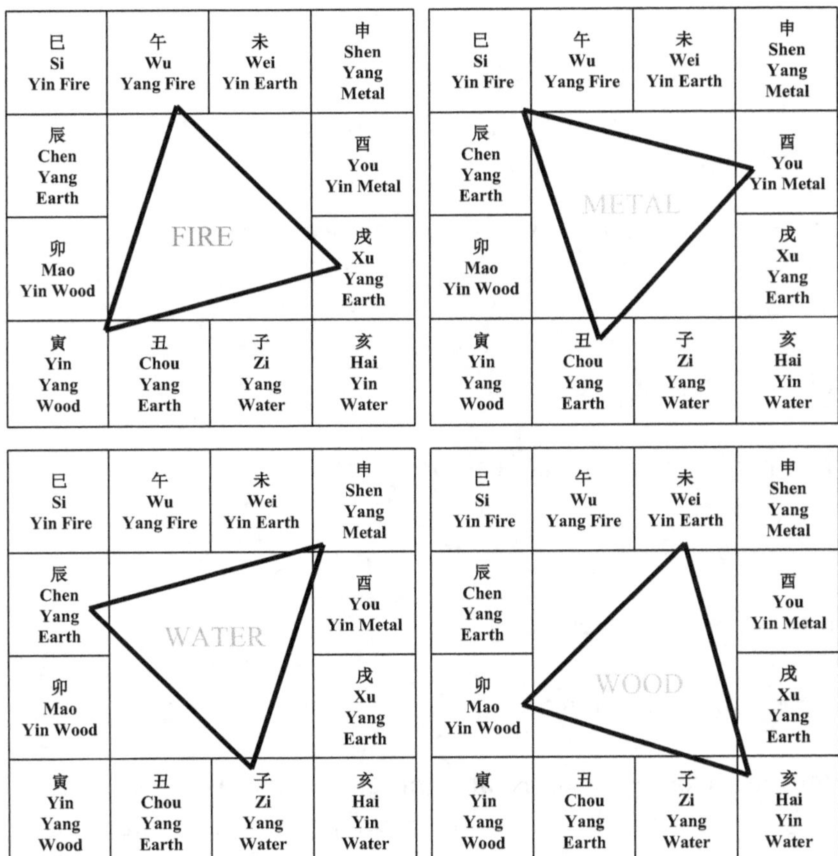

Heaven, Earth and Man 天时, 地利, 人和

The concept of Heaven, Earth and Man (天时, 地利, 人和) is the most important concept in Chinese culture and it has been the cradle of Chinese philosophy for centuries. It is used in all aspect of the Chinese people; starting from basic business transactions, up to warfare and battles of the centuries. Heaven, Earth and Man is also known as 3-Trinity by some Westerners.

Definition of 天时, 地利, 人和

天 – Heaven, sky, season, weather.

时 - Time, season, hour.

天时 – Heaven timing, heavenly time, season, weather.

地 – Earth, land, soil

利 – Favorable, advantageous

地利 – Favourable geographical position.

人 – Human being, people.

和 – Combined, mixed, together.

人和 – Support of people, unity

天时 (Heaven) would mean right timing, good season or good weather. 地利 (Earth) would mean favourable environment or favourable geographical position or condition. In Sun Tzu Art of War, one of the emphasis is to have a favourable geographical position in order to win the war. 人和 would mean the people involved.

In the battle of the Red Cliffs (赤壁之戰), 诸葛亮 Zhuge Liang said: 万事俱备，只欠东风 (All matters are ready, except for east wind). In the battle of Red Cliffs, he wanted to burn up 曹操 (Cáo Cāo)'s fleet of chained ships and knew that it could only be done by launching arrows with fire with the help of the east wind. He used Qi Men (another Feng Shui method) to predict the timing of the east wind so that they can launch the attack. So, this is the 天时 – Heaven aspect. Putting the battle of the Red Cliffs in the Heaven, Earth, Man context:

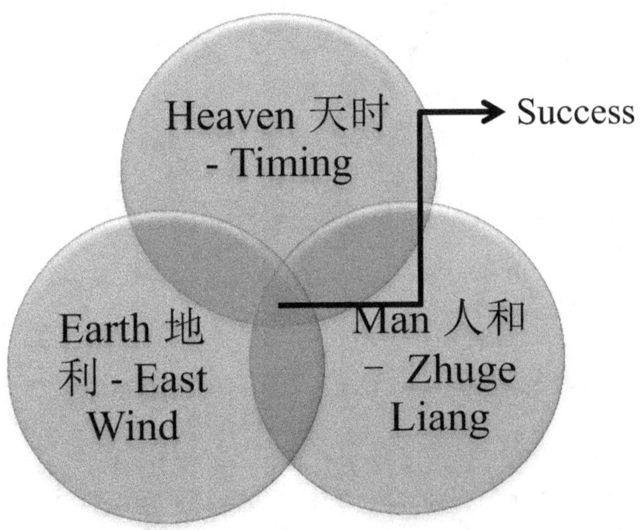

Zhuge Liang and his army (Man 人和), with the help of East Wind (Earth 地利), initiated the battle at the exact timing (Heaven 天时). With this combination, he executed the battle at the right time with the right environment and the correct people. Hence, the success of the battle depended on the quality of these three components as well as the interaction between these three components.

Chinese Meta-Physics concept of Heaven, Earth, Man.

Now we know that to be successful, we need the support of Heaven, Earth and Man (天时、地利、人和). These 3 components have to be in good quality as well as supporting each other in order to ensure success.

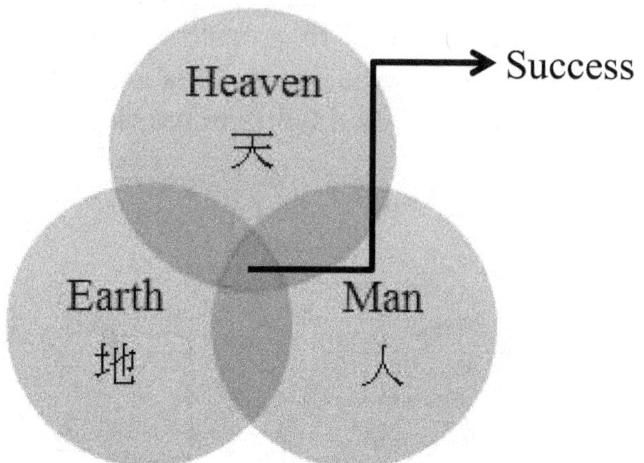

That is why "success" is defined as the overlapping interaction of Heaven, Earth and Man.

Time adjustment or no time adjustment?

As we all know, our current time is adjusted according to our business needs. For example, Singapore is adjusted to GMT+8 even though the actual solar time is GMT+6:55:25. Some countries even have daylight saving, in which the time is added or reduced based on the season. This is to save electricity due to seasonal changes. In divination reading, we plot the chart based on the date and time the person is asking. The time used to plot the chart is based on the time stated on the wall clock. However, in destiny (bazi) reading, some masters adjust the person's birth date and time to the actual solar time. Why is that so? Looking at this in the perspective of Heaven, Earth, Man:

This is where the concept of "Body" and "Use" (体用) comes in. See the Chapter: Concept of Body and Use. Using this concept, you want to see the influence of Heaven and Earth on you. So, Human is "Body" (体), Heaven and Earth is "Use" (用). In other words, we are looking at the Pre-Heaven (先天) information by taking the Human influence out of the equation. When you do this, you need to adjust the date and time based on the actual solar time. Now, you are looking at Pre-Heaven (先天) information about yourself (which is what you are born with).

Since time adjustment is a human action, if you do not adjust the time, you are only looking at the interaction of Heaven, Earth and Man on you. In ancient terms, this is the Post-Heaven (后天) information.

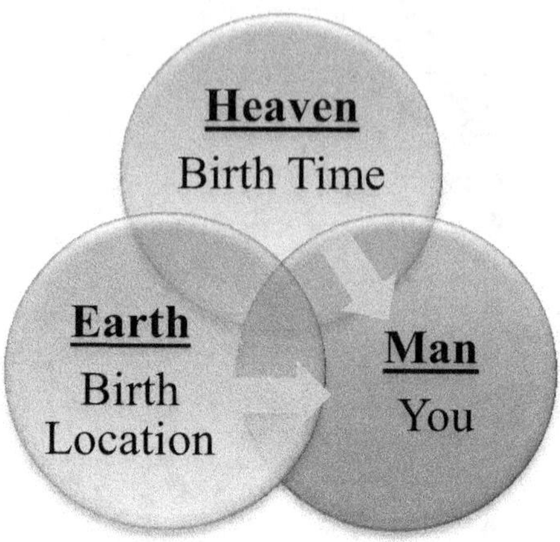

If you are looking at the pure destiny analysis reading, you would then need to use the true Luni-Solar to plot your Zi Wei Dou Shu chart.

Chinese Calendar System

The calendar system that we all know is called the Gregorian calendar, Western calendar, or Christian calendar. It is based on the orbit of the earth around the sun. One year is equivalent to 365.25 days.

The Chinese have 2 calendars; one is called the Lunisolar Calendar and another is called the Xia Calendar/ Solar Calendar/ Farmer Calendar/ JiaZi (甲子) Calendar/ Thousand Years Calendar. The Lunisolar Calendar is based on the cycle of the moon around the earth with adjustment to the Solar Calendar. The first day of the first month of a particular year in Lunisolar Calendar is also known as Chinese New Year.

Lunisolar calendar is based on the new moon. The moon takes approximately 29.5 days to rotate around the Earth. So, a month can consist of 29 or 30 days. A 29 day-month is called a small month, while a 30 day-month is called a big month. Because of this, one Chinese year is shorter by about 10 days. So, after 3 years, an extra month has to be added. To be exact, an extra 7 months are added every 19 years. This is known as the Metonic cycle. These extra 7 months addition is made so that the Spring Equinox always occurs in the 2nd month, the Summer solstice in the 5th month, Autumn Equinox in the 8th Month and Winter Solstice in the 11th Month. This is to ensure that Chinese New Year always falls around Li Chun or the Beginning of Spring.

In Chinese Meta-physics, the Xia Calendar is used. It is called the Xia Calendar because it was invented during the Xia dynasty. It is called Solar Calendar because it is solely based on the orbit of the earth around the sun. It is also called the Farmer Calendar because it indicates the 24 Sub-Season (二十四节气) throughout the year so that farmers know when to start planting and harvesting. As mentioned previously, the indicator of the 24 sub-seasons is based on a certain solar event. For example, Li Chun is when the Sun is at 315^0 in the celestial coordinates.

The key element of Xia Calendar is that it uses the pairing of Heavenly Stem and Earthly Branches to represent the Year, Month, Day and Hour. There are 10 Heavenly Stems – 5 Yang (阳) Stems and 5 Yin (阴) Stems. There are 12 Earthly Branches – 6 Yang (阳) Branches and 6 Yin (阴) Branches. Yang (阳) Stem can only pair with Yang (阳) Branch and Yin (阴) Stem can only pair with Yin (阴) Branch; starting from Jia Zi and ending with Gui Hai, making 60 pairs. Therefore, the pairing is also called **60 JiaZi** (六十甲子). The list of 60 JiaZi (甲子) pairing is as follows:

JiaZi (甲子)	JiaXu (甲戌)	JiaShen (甲申)	JiaWu (甲午)	JiaChen (甲辰)	JiaYin (甲寅)
YiChou (乙丑)	YiHai (乙亥)	YiYou (乙酉)	YiWei (乙未)	YiSi (乙巳)	YiMao (乙卯)
BingYin (丙寅)	BingZi (丙子)	BingXu (丙戌)	BingShen (丙申)	BingWu (丙午)	BingChen (丙辰)
DingMao (丁卯)	DingChou (丁丑)	DingHai (丁亥)	DingYou (丁酉)	DingWei (丁未)	DingSi (丁巳)
WuChen (戊辰)	WuYin (戊寅)	WuZi (戊子)	WuXu (戊戌)	WuShen (戊申)	WuWu (戊午)

JiSi (己巳)	JiMao (己卯)	JiChou (己丑)	JiHai (己亥)	JiYou (己酉)	JiWei (己未)
GengWu (庚午)	GengChen (庚辰)	GengYin (庚寅)	GengZi (庚子)	GengXu (庚戌)	GengShen (庚申)
XinWei (辛未)	XinSi (辛巳)	XinMao (辛卯)	XinChou (辛丑)	XinHai (辛亥)	XinYou (辛酉)
RenShen (壬申)	RenWu (壬午)	RenChen (壬辰)	RenYin (壬寅)	RenZi (壬子)	RenXu (壬戌)
GuiYou (癸酉)	GuiWei (癸未)	GuiSi (癸巳)	GuiMao (癸卯)	GuiChou (癸丑)	GuiHai (癸亥)

Table 1 - 60 JiaZi (甲子)

The Year, Month, Day and Hour runs from Jia Zi to Gui Hai and then starts from Jia Zi again. That is why it is also called Jia Zi Calendar or Thousand Years Calendar, because it never ends.

History of Chinese Calendar

Note: the source of information is from Helmer Aslaksen, Department of Mathematics, National University of Singapore.

http://www.math.nus.edu.sg/aslaksen/calendar/chinese.shtml

Figure 1 - Chinese astronomers determining the summer solstice[1]

The 60-day cycle has been used for keeping track of days since ancient times and it goes back to at least the 13th century BCE during the Shang Dynasty (商朝, 1600–1046 BCE). The 60-month cycle is also very old. The 60-year cycle was introduced during the Han Dynasty (汉朝 202 BCE–220) and is related to the orbital period of Jupiter.

---

[1] http://www.math.nus.edu.sg/aslaksen/calendar/chinese.shtml

Some claim that the calendar was invented by the Yellow Emperor, Huángdì in 2637 BCE during the 61st year of his reign. Some people prefer to start counting from the first year of his reign in 2697 BCE. Since these years are 60 years apart, it follows that 1984 was the first year of either the 78th or 79th 60-year cycle. Using this as a starting point, Chinese New Year in 2000 marks the beginning of the Chinese year 4637 or 4697. Some people write 2636 BCE, but they really mean -2636, using the astronomical year count, where 1 BCE is year 0, 2 BCE is -1, etc.

The continuous year count is not an integral part of the Chinese calendar, but rather, an afterthought. While there are isolated incidents of Chinese scholars who have used it, it only gained popularity with the Jesuit missionaries.

Before 621 BCE, the start of the month was based on visibility of the crescent Moon. During the Zhou (周) dynasty, the Metonic cycle was used for determining leap months and the leap months were always placed at the end of the year. After the Tàichu (太初) calendar reform in 104 BCE, the "no zhongqì" (无中气) rule was used for determining leap months, and the month containing the December solstice was fixed to be the 11th month. The Táng (唐) dynasty calendar reform in 619 switched to follow the true Moon instead. This was inspired by the Indian Buddhist astronomers. The Yuan (元) dynasty reform in 1280 was inspired by Muslim astronomers. The last calendar reform came in 1645 during the Qing dynasty (清) and was implemented by Jesuit missionaries. It used the true Sun. In 1644, the German Adam Schall (Tang Ruowang 汤若望, 1592-1666) went to the new Qing rulers and presented his calculations for an upcoming solar eclipse. He challenged the Chinese and the Muslim astronomers in the Imperial Astronomical Bureau and the Jesuits' calculations were the best. Schall was then appointed director of the Bureau. The next year, he formulated the current rules for the Chinese calendar.

Figure 2 - Adam Schall, Tang Ruowang (汤若望), 1592-1666 (from Wikipedia)

Therefore, the current calendar that we use was reformed by Adam Schall in 1644, where it uses the true Sun path. Any reference to the calendar prior to 1644 is not accurate (that is why it was reformed).

Fundamentals of Zi Wei Dou Shu

The fundamentals of Zi Wei Dou Shu is based on the 12 palaces chart. Example of Princess Diana chart is as follows:

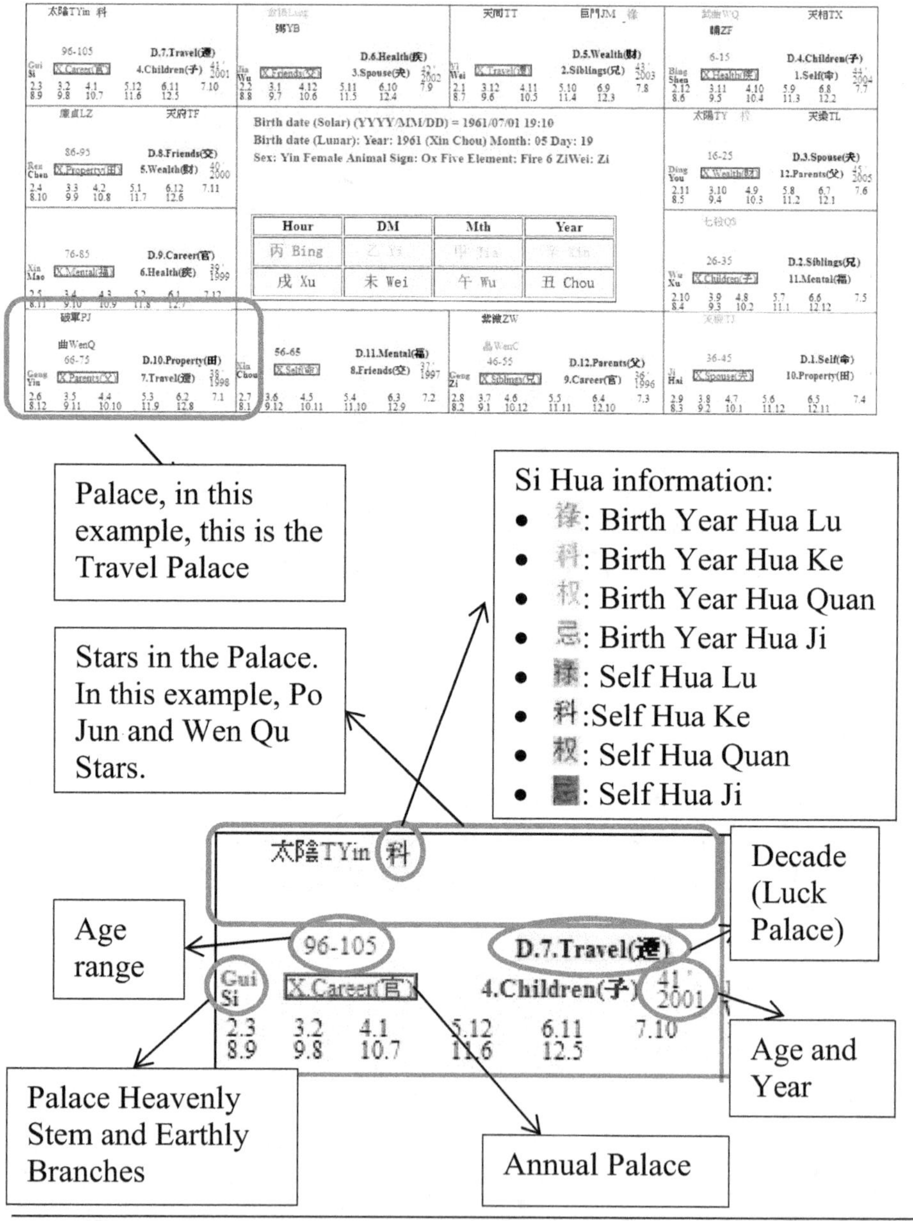

The key to interpreting a Si Hua Zi Wei Dou Shu is based on the flying of Si Hua.

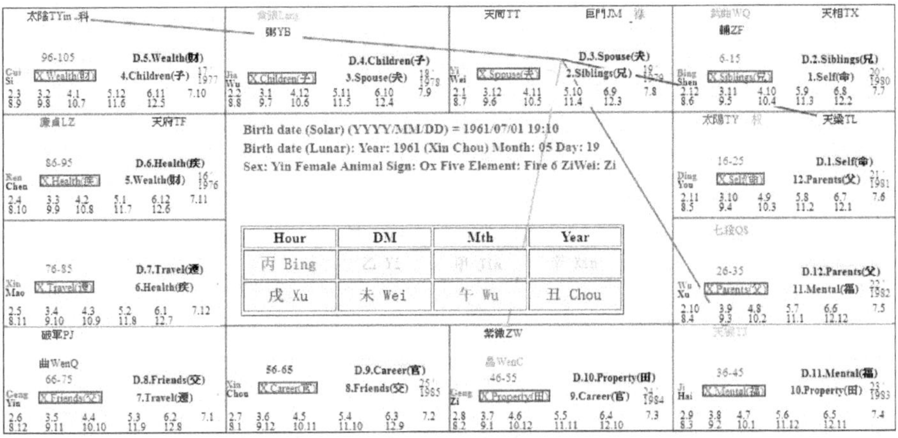

Birth date (Solar) (YYYY/MM/DD) = 1961/07/01 19:10
Birth date (Lunar): Year: 1961 (Xin Chou) Month: 05 Day: 19
Sex: Yin Female Animal Sign: Ox Five Element: Fire 6 ZiWei: Zi

Hour	DM	Mth	Year
丙 Bing	乙 Yi	乙 Yin	辛 Xin
戌 Xu	未 Wei	午 Wu	丑 Chou

For example, Decade Spouse Hua Lu to Property (Tian Ji star), Hua Ji to Children (Tai Yin star), Hua Quan to Parents (Tian Liang star), Hua Ke to Career (Zi Wei star). In 1981, the palace that fly out become Annual Spouse. She got married in 1981.

Pre-Heaven Bagua in Zi Wei Dou Shu chart

The following is the Pre-Heaven Bagua location in a Zi Wei Dou Shu Chart. The attribute of the Pre-Heaven can be used for Zi Wei Dou Shu reading.

Xun	Li	Kun	Kun
Si	Wu	Wei	Shen
Xun			Dui
Chen			You
Zhen			Qian
Mao			Xu
Gen	Gen	Kan	Qian
Yin	Chou	Zi	Hai

Part II – The Ingredient

In this section, the basic attributes of the Si Hua Zi Wei Dou Shu elements are presented.

18 Stars of Zi Wei Dou Shu

In the Si Hua lineage of Zi Wei Dou Shu, a total of 14 main stars and 4 auxiliary stars are used.

The 14 main stars are:

Star	Category	Element
Zi Wei (紫微)	Northern	Yin Earth
Wu Qu (武曲)	Northern	Yin Metal
Lian Zhen (廉贞)	Northern	Yin Fire
Tan Lang (贪狼)	Northern	Yang Wood (root: Yin Water)
Ju Men (巨门)	Northern	Yin Water
Po Jun (破军)	Northern	Yin Water
Tian Ji (天机)	Southern	Yin Wood
Tian Tong (天同)	Southern	Yang Water
Tian Liang (天梁)	Southern	Yang Earth
Qi Sha (七杀)	Southern	Yang Metal
Tian Fu (天府)	Southern	Yang Earth
Tian Xiang (天相)	Southern	Yang Water
Tai Yang (太阳)	Middle	Yang Fire
Tai Yin (太阴)	Middle	Yin Water

4 Auxiliary stars are:

Star
Wen Chang (文昌)
Wen Qu (文曲)
Zuo Fu (左辅)
You Bi (右弼)

Zi Wei (紫微)

Category	Description
Star	Northern Star
5-Element	Yin Earth
Heavenly Stem	Ji Earth
Overview	Honourable, a beautiful mountain
Basic Characteristics	Emperor, high class, high and mighty, lonely, only looks good but words do not carry weight, prideful. Authoritative / controlling, benevolent, lucky, has good fortune
Governs	Career that is nominated by others (like an elected emperor or a person born with privilege)
Strength(s)	ZiWei star is a leadership star, and has the air of a leader- strong self-respect, filial and emotional. They like to lead everything, and do not feel secure when other people decide for him/her. When issuing commands, he/she will know the direction to move forward. As this is how they think and execute, it is why they have the potential to be capable leaders. They will take care of weaker people because they believe that they have the ability to do so and are superior to them, not because they sympathise them.
Weakness(es)	The characteristics of ZiWei people is that they are self-centric, a bit petty, sometimes a bit childish, and attention-seekers. They are egoistic, like to be bootlicked, easily influenced by others and fickle-minded.
Self Palace	ZiWei at Self Palace means that the person wants face and has self-confidence. In the situation that he/she is being neglected, he/she will not be able to take it. They think that they are the king, and no matter what type of king they are, they cannot accept being neglected. Unless all of them are kings, then it will be like an assembly of heroes, in which they would all party together.

	ZiWei at Self Palace means that the person would be easily influenced by other stars. This means that some of them would be introverts, some extroverts, some with very strong (character), some that are pessimistic. In addition, they have a strong willpower, but are also very concerned about their external appearance. People with the ZiWei star likes to pay attention to others but also want others to pay attention to them as well. They are like a beautiful mountain that requires the admiration from others. This can be seen in their character as well, in which both the male and the female would like to dress up. For both the males and the females, they would not allow him/herself to become too fat as they would feel the need to look beautiful.
Relationship(s)	They preferred to be pampered, so the partner of a person with ZiWei in Self Palace would need to be very romantic. Those with Zi Wei in Self Palace would need to be careful so as to not be conned by others. This is because they are very emotional and would easily get in trouble due to their emotions. For example, they may have a new partner, but may still decide to take care of their old partner, and this would cause an emotional roller coaster for them. They are very concerned about how people look at them, and at times are easily suspicious of others. In addition, they are easily conned by others that speak sweetly to them.
Si Hua	Hua Quan (Ren) – Produce Me Hua Ke (Yi) – Restrict Me

Wu Qu (武曲)

Category	Description
Star	Northern Star
5-Element	Yin Metal
Heavenly Stem	Xin Metal
Overview	Sacrifice, steadfast, rigid.
Basic Characteristics	Underground Metal; need to dig out and be refined before it can be used. Although it governs Wealth, it does not mean that the person will have wealth when it is at the Wealth Palace. This is because it needs to be refined before it can be used. In addition, the Career Palace has to be good as well. It also represents Solitary/Widow Star.
Governs	Wealth (But need to put in effort to gain wealth)
Strength(s)	Steadfast and never say die attitude. They are hardworking and will not slack.
Weakness(es)	They want things to happen immediately, and are like a turning gear that cannot stop. They are also very rigid in handling matters. They emphasise on material stuff. They are not very good in handling relationships, so sometimes Wu Qu is also known as the solitary/widow star.
Self Palace	Wu Qu is a diligent star, and the person's character is diligent, straightforward, steadfast, impatient, has personality and is loyal to his/her friends. Wu Qu at Self represents someone who is hardworking, and no matter what, they will have a strong will power. They are unlikely to make- up or do up themselves, and when you see them, that is their real face. They cannot lie. For the male chart: they have the ability to put things into motion, and are daring and optimistic. For the female chart: they will go against their own desire, their whole life will be laborious, they will be a loner, conservative, and will not easily ask for help.
Relationship(s)	They are more interested in making money than being in a relationship. Others will think that Wu

	Qu people are not romantic, but they actually want a fast type of relationship; fast start, fast finish. It does not mean that they do not love their partner, it is just that they do not know how to express their love. They would rather make more money than to spend time in a courtship. They have problems expressing themselves as well, so being in a relationship with them would be filled with misunderstandings. Although they are not suitable in handling love matters, but they are trustworthy and hardworking and good at socializing, so they will be admired by others in the business world. They strongly value promises, so you better keep your promises to them.
Si Hua	Hua Lu (Ji) – Support Me Hua Quan (Geng) – Restrict Me Hua Ke (Jia) – I restrict Hua Ji (Ren) – I produce

Lian Zhen (廉贞)

Category	Description
Star	Northern Star
5-Element	Yin Fire
Heavenly Stem	Ding Fire
Overview	Imprisonment, law & order, need to/ will put in effort, a volcano waiting to erupt.
Basic Characteristics	Represents law and order, being controlled and confined (imprisoned)
Governs	Career
Strength(s)	Leadership and agile. Good human to human relationship. Extroverted, lively and outgoing.
Weakness(es)	Lian Zhen Star has leadership abilities, and they have a very strong character and are strong minded, sometimes a bit stubborn. Their feelings can flip from good to bad quickly, and it is not easy to understand their character. They can be viewed as outspoken and cocky.
Self Palace	Lian Zhen is like a peaceful but active volcano. It looks peaceful because there is a lot of energy cannot be released. However, when the energy is released, aka, when they have achieved something, they want people to think highly of them and praise them. They are born leaders, extroverted, and are very good at human relationship management. Although they look outgoing, but internally, they also need their quiet and personal space for thinking and to recharge. When they are younger they could be introverts, but when they grow up, they become extroverts. Lian Zhen at Self is someone who has an agile mind and is intelligent. They like freedom, so they are very good at dodging troublesome

	matters. Lian Zhen people like to doll themselves up and spend money on make-up. They have good PR and planning skills. They like freedom and will not concern themselves with small matters. They do not like to be controlled by others, and are frank and outspoken. Lian Zhen also means to imprison, so they tend to have self-imprisoning characteristics. Although they are lively and extroverted, internally, they feel lonely and often keep to themselves.
Relationship(s)	They have a good relationship with the opposite sex. They have strong desire for love. For some, this desire is due to the fact that they want to own the person (possessive). You will be very happy with them as they will be very involved in the relationship. But as their mindset of love is to play, their partner needs to be able to accept that.
Si Hua	Hua Lu (Jia) – I restrict Hua Ji (Bing) – Restrict Me

Tan Lang (贪狼)

Category	Description
Star	Northern Star
5-Element	Yang Wood
Heavenly Stem	Jia Wood, root is Gui Water
Overview	Longevity, education, wealth, flirtatious feeling, likes freedom (carefree), enjoyment, education, spiritual, middle man. Chinese Meta-Physics.
Basic Characteristics	Tan Lang is like a free flow of the wind, and Tan Lang people likes freedom and enjoyment. Therefore, people with the Tan Lang Star gives others a good first impression. They are also very good at socializing, especially with the opposite sex. They also have a carefree type of character (Flamboyant).
Governs	Mental
Strength(s)	Tan Lang is agile, and as they have a strong urge to study, they look for continuous education. They are not reserved when doing things, and are adaptable to change. They like to interact with others, and will be bored if they are alone. Tang Lang people are compassionate, extroverted, they will not stay still, have a lot of desire, have a fierce character and likes do things fast.
Weakness(es)	They like to dream and they like unrealistic things. Male chart: potential to be a gambler and lazy. Female chart: potential to get pregnant before getting married.
Self Palace	For people with Tan Lang at Self, they have the desire to be at the centre of attention and they are suitable and have the energy to be in the service industry. Tan Lang is also a peach blossom star but it all depends on the Si Hua. Tan Lang people likes to use brain power, and they like tasks that requires a lot of brain power.

	Therefore, this person is also very knowledgeable. However, they do not spend a lot of time doing deep research, which means that they are likely to have general knowledge of everything but is a master of none.
Relationship(s)	Their social circle needs to be very active as socializing is very important to them. Therefore, they will spend a lot of money on make-up, shopping, and things than enables them to enjoy life or socialise. Tan Lang people are flirtatious, likes to sweet talk, and is also good at sweet talking others. They like to explore unconventional types of relationships (affairs, same-sex relationships etc).
Si Hua	Hua Lu (Wu) – Restrict Me Hua Quan (Ji) – I produce Hua Ji (Gui) – Produce Me

Ju Men (巨门)

Category	Description
Star	Northern Star
5-Element	Yin Water
Heavenly Stem	Gui Water
Overview	Hidden, dark/gloomy, outspoken, gossip, scandals, need to cultivate in order to have returns.
Basic Characteristics	Insecurity complex, things related to the mouth, hidden agenda, gourmet luck.
Governs	Wealth
Strength(s)	The Ju Men Star is like a big earth, and it needs sunlight to create a beautiful picture. The optimistic part of Ju Men Star will give people a sense of security, but the restless part of Ju Men star will cause people to distance themselves from them. Therefore, the good and bad aspect of Ju Men is a bit of contradicting, and the good and bad aspects depends on their internal thinking. If they are optimistic in facing the situation, others will be able to feel it too. Ju Men people are sharp, observant and have good endurance. They are good in analysis and strong in research.
Weakness(es)	Their weakness is in the way that they communicate, as they are very direct and do not know how to sugar coat. They draw a clear line between business and personal matters. If the matter is about business, then it has to be strictly business. If matter is personal, then as long as you are a good friend, everything can be settled. They do not like to socialise, so it is very difficult to understand what they are thinking. It is also very difficult to buy over a Ju Men person, which is both a good and bad aspect of their character. They are good at predicting other people's thoughts and

	actions, which means that every social event with them might have a motive behind it. Therefore, Ju Men people might not have many friends. They are very meticulous in handling matters, but because of their intelligence, they are always unhappy with the abilities of the people around them. As such, they often are viewed as arrogant and selfish.
Self Palace	Ju Men is an inner struggle star. They are attentive, not very good in articulating, secretive and they get into trouble easily. People with the Ju Men star are confident, eloquent and intelligent, but their intelligence is not used in their communication with others. They are sometimes too straightforward and do not know how to be subtle and politically correct. Although they are eloquent, they are not very good in delivering the message in a subtle manner, and this will get them into trouble most of the time. To them, it is a straightforward matter, but it does not sit well to others. They are inclined to a career in research .
Relationship(s)	They have a very strong endurance. They are very observant, so they have a strong and suspicious mind. They like to be alone and are likely to be introverts that focuses on protecting themselves due to their suspicious minds. Normally, it is not easy to have such friend, but if they are really your friend, then they will be your close comrade. Of course, you would need to open up their heart and fully understand them first before they can become your true friend (as they are suspicious in nature).
Si Hua	Hua Lu (Xin) – Produce me Hua Quan (Gui) – I restrict Hua Ji (Ding) – support me

Po Jun (破军)

Category	Description
Star	Northern Star
5-Element	Yin Water
Heavenly Stem	Gui Water
Overview	Responsible, solitary, restricting, a surging ocean. Represents Husband, son or slave.
Basic Characteristics	Destroyer that first destroys before becoming good. Energy draining, keeps changing mind, likes fresh stuff, impatient, a lot of selfish desire, eager to do things, will not admit defeat and has a high desire for revenge.
Governs	Children
Strength(s)	They like the process of execution but do not like to follow the process step by step. Po Jun star is an entrepreneur star. They have leadership abilities, such as an energetic and vigorous character. They are straightforward, and are not suitable to do things that requires planning. Their character is kind hearted, intelligent, agile, and eloquent but they like to argue. They are very good at adapting to situations and are fast in reacting. But at the same time, they are impatient, and wanting to succeed is what drives them their entire life.
Weakness(es)	They are unable to stop and listen. As they are bad at planning, they will execute without thinking. Even there is a plan, they will only take into consideration the first half of the plan. They also will not bother to make a backup plan. They might also rush in get things done fast. They will strive for a perfect world and may sometimes be eccentric. Most of the time, they

	would have achieved success but they might neglect their own family members in the process. They are also always suspicious about everything and are also arrogant in nature.
Self Palace	People with Po Jun at self are like a surging ocean, sometimes calm, and sometimes they are like a tsunami. But, just like how the ocean's waves are a result of the moon's movement, people with Po Jun is not may not be aware of the situation themselves. It is not easy to understand them, so the best way is to allow them to have their own space. If they encounter any constraints, it will prevent them from manifesting their talent. When they are young, they like to move about (cannot sit still). They are extroverts that enjoy making new friends and likes disturbing their friends. The Po Jun star is also a consumption star, so they consume a lot of energy. When Po Jun is at the Self Palace, they may get injured easily, and their parents need to take extra precautions. Because of their nature, it is not possible to ask them to sit down quietly. Therefore, they are suitable for an entrepreneurial type of career. If they are asked to do a mundane type of work, then it will be a problem. They will also need to fail first before they can succeed. Furthermore, they like to create new environments. For example, they are the type of people that would rebuild the country after a long war.
Relationship(s)	They like to make friends and are loyal to their friends. However, they do not know how to choose good friends, and are often sabotaged by their friends.
Si Hua	Hua Lu (Gui) – Produce Me Hua Quan (Jia) – I restrict

Tian Ji (天机)

Category	Description
Star	Southern Star
5-Element	Yin Wood
Heavenly Stem	Yi Wood
Overview	Longevity, perseverance, unaffected by setbacks, advisor, marketing. Objects it represents: Mirror, stairs, chariot, curtain, door
Basic Characteristics	Always have a motive, continuous movement, same social status, not straightforward. Likes Chinese Meta-Physics, religion or philosophy.
Governs	Sibling or someone with the same social status.
Strength(s)	Tian Ji is like a small plant in spring, even in a very dire situation, it can still survive. They are very confident, especially for those that have gone through a lot of hardship. They have strong sense of self-confidence and perseverance. However, they cannot handle their own shortcomings.
Weakness(es)	They like to move about and are sceptical, rash and impatient. It might seem easy to get along with them, but they will ultimately always protect themselves first. So, when criticized, they will strongly fight back. They will not follow the norm and sometimes take short cuts. They will always have a reason or intent behind their actions.
Self Palace	They will look down on those who are slow in thinking as they are able to think fast. They have a strong analytical mind but lack the charisma of a leader. So they tend to lose out when starting a new business. They like to be in fast- changing and competitive situations, but prefer not to be a boss as

	they do not want to be involved in the financial aspects of the company. They are suitable for sales and work that involves planning, thinking and analysis. They are able to grasp things fast, but cannot accept being criticized by others. Thus, they are both loved and hated. Tian Ji people need to put themselves in the shoes of others and start thinking about the outcome of their actions. This might help them be more creative as well.
Relationship(s)	They are very sentimental, and therefore fall in love easily. This may lead to problems when they fall in love with multiple people at the same time. Furthermore, due to their perseverance, they are very focused in their relationships.
Si Hua	Hua Lu (Yi) – Restrict Me Hua Quan (Bing) – I produce Hua Ke (Ding) – Support Me Hua Ji (Wu) – Produce Me

Tian Tong (天同)

Category	Description
Star	Southern Star
5-Element	Yang Water
Heavenly Stem	Ren Water
Overview	Feeling of idling, playful character, joyful life, lucky, longevity, emotional, acting like a small kid.
Basic Characteristics	Tian Tong Star can only be happy when they are enjoying life. This type of enjoyment could be: watching TV, watching movie, eating and drinking. They need to find time to celebrate life in order to be able to move forward.
Governs	Mental
Strength(s)	Very good communicator and have very young/ childlike features (boyish/girlish look). They are very emotional, so it is hard to reason with them when it comes to emotional matters. Tian Tong is a leisure star that has a gentle and compassionate heart. Tian Tong is also a good fortune star because they can easily forget about their troubles and continue to enjoy life. They prefers stability, and are suitable to handle stable matters. They do not have the characteristics of an entrepreneur.
Weakness(es)	They do not like to follow the rules and do not like to be controlled. They are temperamental, wilful, emotional and lack focus. They are the ones who would cry while watching a sad movie. At times, they can be childish as well. They will only work on matters when there is no choice.
Self Palace	For people with Tian Tong at Self, they will always have people taking care of them for their whole life. As they like to enjoy life, they would not go and

	fight very hard for money. Therefore, it might seem like they do not care about material things. For females, as they like to hear compliments, they might go for plastic surgery.
Relationship(s)	They are very emotional, and like to love and be loved. They get hurt easily as they are emotional. They are also usually too involved in the ideals of romance and forget about reality. They look for real love.
Si Hua	Hua Lu (Bing) – Produce Me Hua Quan (Ding) – I restrict Hua Ji (Geng) – Support Me

Tian Liang (天梁)

Category	Description
Star	Southern Star
5-Element	Yang Earth
Heavenly Stem	Wu Earth
Overview	Human relationships, high cloud, taking care of people (like an elderly person taking care of the young)
Basic Characteristics	Knowledgeable, resourceful, gossip, longevity, likes to nag. Ability to turn inauspicious into auspicious (逢凶化吉). Need to experience calamity before becoming good.
Governs	Parent
Strength(s)	Tian Liang is an honest and frank star. They are honest and upright, straightforward, mature and warm-hearted. Tian Liang is like the earth's high cloud. Therefore, they are mature, frank, upright, experienced, and will not be shy in social situations. They are very good at socializing. They also like to take care of others and be taken care of.
Weakness(es)	They think highly of themselves because they have a long-term perspective of things. However, this may cause problems and gossip when they interact with others. They are also temperamental and likes to show-off. Most of the time, they like to put people down.
Self Palace	People with Tian Liang at Self Palace think highly of themselves, and have a refined type character. They are not fickle and once they make up their mind, they will go ahead to do it. They are normally eloquent and like to discuss or argue with others. Tian Liang is also known as the Old Man Star. This means that they will mature early and have affinity

	with elders. They have a strong analytical and leadership skills. They see things only from their point of view, and they tend to be stubborn, which might lead to communication issues. For people with Tian Liang at Self, they need to experience and overcome hardships before getting good returns (turning inauspicious into auspicious (逢凶化吉))
Relationship(s)	People with Tian Liang at Self Palace do not waste time on mundane matters. For example, if their house is a bit messy, they might not clean up the house as they do not think that it is important. They will not take initiative in their relationships. As they like to argue, their partner might have a difficult time, so it is necessary for their partner to properly understand them. They are temperamental against others, objective in handling matters, farsighted, capable, likes showing off and putting other people down. Therefore, they do not have many friends.
Si Hua	Hua Lu (Ren) – I produce Hua Quan (Yi) – Produce Me Hua Ke (Ji) - Restrict Me

Qi Sha (七杀)

Category	Description
Star	Southern Star
5-Element	Yang Metal
Heavenly Stem	Geng Metal
Overview	Courage, sharp knife, forging ahead, solitary.
Basic Characteristics	Like sharp knife, their abilities are already obvious, so there is no need for others to compliment them. Competitive, intelligent, capable, artistically inclined and righteous. Impatient, likes to look down on others and does not like talking much.
Governs	None.
Strength(s)	They are mature, will not hesitate to take on challenges, and will not give up. They are hardworking, courageous and have an explosive character. When they decide on a matter, it is like a fired arrow, and they will forge ahead. Internally, they like to be encouraged and complimented, just like how the wind helps to push the arrow forward, determined to hit the target. Qi Sha people are very stable and have a strong will.
Weakness(es)	They get excited easily, and might be a bit inflexible and stubborn. If you are a bit slow or not hardworking enough, you might be intimated by Qi Sha people. Qi Sha Star is the star that likes to put others down.
Self Palace	For people with Qi Sha Star at Self Palace, they emphasise a lot on being capable. Therefore, these people are also those that work very hard. Their character is also intimidating, as they will speak their mind and will not care about how other people feel. Thus, they are not good in dealing with people- related issues. However, their temperament

	will come fast and go fast. They have high expectation of themselves as well as others. If you are their subordinate or child, you might feel like you are in in a military training camp. As they like to do things fast, they are likely to make a lot of mistakes. Thus, they should learn to slow down and have patience. E.g They could embark on a spiritual journey.
Relationship(s)	They believe in love at first sight and want to get it over and done with. They do not want to drag it out for too long. However, their strong character might cause problems as well, as they will work hard to support the family but neglect the family at the same time. It is good for them to be married late. This is because this is a primary talent star, meaning that they will need to work hard for their career. If they marry early, they might end up sacrificing their marriage for their career.
Si Hua	Nil

Tian Fu (天府)

Category	Description
Star	Southern Star
5-Element	Yang Earth
Heavenly Stem	Wu Earth
Overview	If Zi Wei = Emperor, Tian Fu = Queen, then Tian Fu represents the people who take care of matters that are inside the palace. Inheritance, a very hard stone, conservative, firm. Tian Fu is like a CEO of a company that manages other people's money.
Basic Characteristics	Represents 衣食住行 (yī shí zhù xíng), clothing, food, shelter and means of travel. Agriculture, farming and entertainment.
Governs	Property/Wealth
Strength(s)	Tian Fu Star represents strength and willpower. They are like a very hard stone, and they have their own thinking. They will not be easily compromised, and it will be difficult to change their minds. They will be very good to their own children. Although they may not be very good in talking/ communicating, but they will protect their family members. They are stable, impatient and responsible. As they have high self-confidence, they have a strong feeling of superiority. When issuing a command, it gives them a sense of achievement.
Weakness(es)	They have the problem of loving someone too much and are overly concerned about them. They have good intentions and only want others to be good, just like a parent's love to their children. However, their technique of expressing it is not

	good. They are impatient. They always look for perfection as they always want to achieve a "perfect world". Furthermore, for important stuff, they will need to do it immediately, otherwise they will not be able to stand it. They like to order people around but do not like to be the lead.
Self Palace	They emphasise a lot on money. Therefore, they are the type that will save money. However, they will sometimes spend a lot of money, and sometimes they will be calculative. Tian Fu star is also known as the Heavenly Kitchen star, and they have gourmet luck and likes to eat. However, they are not the one that is cooking, but rather, they are the who is judging the food. If they start to gain weight, it means that their wealth luck has arrived. Female chart: Noble, temperamental and elegant.
Relationship(s)	Tian Fu Star people are sensible because they want to be in command, but if their potential partners are not people that listen to their commands, then they may sometimes get disappointed in the relationship. This is because they have a big ego, and they need someone to give in to them.
Si Hua	Nil

Tian Xiang (天相)

Category	Description
Star	Southern Star
5-Element	Yang Water
Heavenly Stem	Ren Water
Overview	Quiet lake, full of wisdom, nosy, follows order (no leadership quality), kind, amiable.
Basic Characteristics	Tian Xiang is like a quite lake inside the mountain, in which there is an emphasis on image and internal knowledge. It represents 衣食住行 (yī shí zhù xíng), clothing, food, shelter and means of travel. Like the secretary of a boss, Tian Xiang is a holder of the seal but with no power.
Governs	Basic necessities.
Strength(s)	They are happy to acquire knowledge. They emphasis more on the quality than the quantity and therefore, they will create things that are of high quality. They will always need to need to know the reason behind something, and will sacrifice anything for it. Sometimes, they are like nagging parents, but they have good intentions. They are gentle, have a good temperament, easy going and likes to help others. They are humorous and likes to say things that other people like to hear. They are well-liked by others, and have good interpersonal relationships. They can make friends with people who have power and status.
Weakness(es)	They have the tendency to show- off. The problem is that their method of showing off can be over-the-top. It is not that they are bad at communicating, but it is because people are not able to understand their expectations.
Self Palace	Tian Xiang is a service star, and people with Tian Xiang at the Self Palace have the enthusiasm to

	provide service and fight for justice and fairness. They are also loyal, intelligent, compassionate, and indecisive. When Tian Xiang is at Self, the Qi Sha Star will be at the Mental Palace, and this means that it will be difficult for them to relax. They will take on straining and difficult jobs, and even if they may not be good at it, they will still go ahead and do it. Those with Tian Xiang star will feel very vexed and overworked. Sometimes when there are things that no one is doing/ no one wants to do, they will take it up.
Relationship(s)	They are too sympathetic and it is a disadvantage to them in our current society that is full of corruption and deceit. They will easily spend money and are easily convinced by others, so they need to be careful of being scammed in a relationship.
Si Hua	Nil

Tai Yang (太阳)

Category	Description
Star	Middle Star
5-Element	Yang Fire
Heavenly Stem	Bing Fire
Overview	Tribute, busy sun, always giving, generous, optimistic, easily conned, over-bearing and warmth.
Basic Characteristics	Tai Yang people are optimistic, hardworking and steady. They are like the sun that does not care about the wind or the rain. They emphasis a lot on efficiency and rules, but they also admire those who work hard, as they believe that anything can be accomplished with hard work. They are willing to sacrifice themselves for things that they love and want to do.
Governs	Career (gained from competition), Father, Husband (Female chart), Male
Strength(s)	They are good helpers as they are hardworking, loyal, filial, compassionate, generous and noble They will take care of their family and will sacrifice themselves for others to shine. They are loyal and filled with "brotherly love". Thus, they will not hesitate to sacrifice themselves for others.
Weakness(es)	For things that they are interested in, if they feel that the environment (E.g people) or progress is draggy or slow, they will not like it. Since they are generous, they can be easily conned or over-commit to something.
Self Palace	Tai Yang Star is a tribute star. They are enthusiastic, loyal, filial and compassionate. They will also take care of their family and will not hesitate to sacrifice themselves for others to shine. They are also impulsive and impatient. They are hardworking people and will not hesitate to put in

	100% effort. They are very hardworking and are likely to be workaholics. They can be straightforward, warm, enthusiastic, generous and easily jealous. They are also very ambitious.
Relationship(s)	They are impulsive and tend to say things that will hurt others. This is one problem that they need to take note of. They are also like the sun and will not hesitate to sacrifice (burn) themselves. They will not beat around the bush to make you happy. Tai Yang female is a "home nobleman", which means that they will take charge and take care of the house. Tai Yang Male emphasises a lot on career as compared to a Tai Yang Female. A Tai Yang Female will emphasise more on family but a Tai Yang Male will probably work too hard and neglect the family. In any case, for both the male and the female, they will go for fame and status in their careers.
Si Hua	Hua Lu (Geng) – I restrict Hua Quan (Xin) – Support Me Hua Ji (Jia) – Restrict Me

Tai Yin (太阴)

Category	Description
Star	Middle Star
5-Element	Yin Water
Heavenly Stem	Gui Water
Overview	Tai Yin star is like the moon in the sky, although it is clear and bright but it is still subjected to change. Represents things that are related to the night.
Basic Characteristics	Tai Yin people will be satisfied when others are shining. Therefore, they will often sacrifice themselves, especially for their family members.
Governs	Property, Wife (Male chart), Female, Daughter, Mother
Strength(s)	Tai Yin is a gentle star, and the person is gentle, caring, sentimental, conservative and will not like to compete. Tai Yin is also a Mother Star, and just like a mother, people with Tai Yin Star are gentle, filial and will take care of their family. They are spiritual people, and will work towards spiritual fulfilment. They will also prefer to stay in a single place as they are sentimental people. Therefore, when working, they will not go and fight for power. However, because of their capability, they are often put in charge. Tai Yin is also a Wealth Star. A wealth star will know how to save money. Regardless of high or low income, they will be able to save to increase their wealth.
Weakness(es)	They like to dream and are nosy. They emphasise a lot on other people, and their emotions will fluctuate depending on how others see them. They will also stick to their principals and have

	fixed beliefs. Although they are gentle, but they are also stubborn. They can be impatient and are easily jealous.
Self Palace	They are impatient but they will work slowly. This is because they emphasise a lot on quality, and also only do things when they feel like it, so people might think that they are inefficient. However, they are very artistic, so even though they are slow, producing quality output is their forte. They can be emotional as they keep everything to themselves and will not want to say it out. Potentially, their father may have 2 wives or they may have a god-mother. Male Chart: Good relationship with people of the opposite sex as they are very gentle.
Relationship(s)	Because of the way they live their life, they will be gentle and elegant. They will take care of their family, and will be busy as they will spend most of their time taking care of their family. They are the "family nobleman", and will take care of the family. They will normally sacrifice more than what they will gain.
Si Hua	Hua Lu (Ding) – Produce Me Hua Quan (Wu) – I restrict Hua Ke (Geng) – I produce Hua Ji (Yi) – Support Me

Wen Chang (文昌)

Category	Description
Star	Southern Star
5-Element	Yang Metal
Heavenly Stem	Geng
Overview	Wen Chang represents academic studies, reputation, artistic talent, refined character.
Basic Characteristics	Gentle appearance, graceful and good temperament. Gives people the impression of well- mannered and learned person.
Governs	Academics
Strength(s)	Their thinking is systematic and refined. They are intelligent, has a strong, analytical and agile mind, and are eloquent and humorous. Strong and has talent in the Academics (studies).
Weakness(es)	They are too knowledgeable, and may come off as cocky and a show- off. Sometimes, they lack EQ in handling matters.
Self Palace	They have high IQ and are versatile with a good memory. They are talented and are good academically.
Relationship(s)	They like the process and courtship in their relationship(s) but do not like the commitment. Thus, their family members and spouse needs to be understanding and patient with them.
Si Hua	Hua Ke (Bing) – I restrict Hua Ji (Xin) – I produce

Wen Qu (文曲)

Category	Description
Star	Northern Star
5-Element	Yin Water
Heavenly Stem	Gui
Overview	Represents soft, gentle, mild, eloquent, elegant, refined and gentle.
Basic Characteristics	They are eloquent and gifted in performing and music. They are sensitive of other people's feelings when they talk to them, and are emotional people. They have similar characteristics as the Wen Chang Star, as they are both learning stars. However, the Wen Chang star represents the more conventional forms of studying, whereas the Wen Qu star represents the arts, the art of talking and inner thinking.
Governs	Arts
Strength(s)	They are eloquent, versatile and gentle. They are artistically talented and good at performing. They come off as people with high EQ.
Weakness(es)	As they are eloquent, they might sometimes overdo it and come off as arrogant. They may also be overly engrossed in their art and tend to be disconnected from the outside world.
Self Palace	They are smart, knowledgeable and versatile. They are artistically talented and good at the performing arts or music.
Relationship(s)	They tend to be more emotional in their relationships and can be very romantic. They might not take it well when the other party wants to break-up.
Si Hua	Hua Ke (Xin) – I produce Hua Ji (Ji) – Support Me

Zuo Fu (左輔)

Category	Description
Star	Northern Star
5-Element	Yang Earth
Heavenly Stem	Wu
Overview	Zuo Fu represents sincerity and kindness. It is the nobleman star and the assistance star. Skilful and generous, easy going, admirable, the desire to be better, has aspirations.
Basic Characteristics	Smart and intelligent, has strategy, honest and upright, generous and dependable. Good nature and have good human relationships.
Governs	Loyalty.
Strength(s)	Loyal and righteous, generous, easy-going, self-motivated and ambitious. They are smart, clever, strategic, honest, generous, practical, inclusive, repetitive and good.
Weakness(es)	They can sometimes be overly protective of their friends or relatives and this will cause problem for them. For example, they will be willing to bear the consequences of the wrongdoings of their friends or relatives.
Self Palace	Single Star at Self without any major star – They will respect their parents.
Relationship(s)	They will always think about their past relationships. They are also emotional, and will cherish their relationships.
Si Hua	Hua Ke (Ren) – Restrict Me

You Bi (右弼)

Category	Description
Star	Northern Star
5-Element	Yin Water
Heavenly Stem	Gui
Overview	You Bi represents an open mind. It is a Nobleman star and an Assistance star.
Basic Characteristics	They are autocratic, intelligent, emotional, capable, quick-witted, and always aspire to be the best. They are honest, frank, good at writing and executing plans, and they do things very carefully and strategically.
Governs	Loyalty.
Strength(s)	They are open, smart, capable, witty, self-motivated and ambitious.
Weakness(es)	They can be emotional and sometimes overbearing.
Self Palace	They are loyal, honest, compassionate and good at planning and execution.
Relationship(s)	They tend to be emotional and easily distracted in their relationships.
Si Hua	Hua Ke (Wu) – I produce

12 Palaces of Zi Wei Dou Shu

The 12 Palaces of Zi Wei Dou Shu are arranged in an anti-clockwise pattern starting from the Self Palace: Self → Siblings → Spouse → Children → Wealth → Health → Travel → Friends → Career → Property → Mental → Parents.

If you assign a number to each palace, then palace 1 (Self), 5 (Wealth) and 9 (Career) will form a triangle called the San He Triangle. Opposite of Self (1) is Travel (7), and all together, they form what is called the "3 Triangle and 4 Middle" (三方四正) as seen below:

Gui Si Siblings	Jia Wu Self	Yi Wei Parents	Bing Shen Mental
Ren Chen Spouse			Ding You Property
Xin Mao Children			Wu Xu Career
Geng Yin Wealth	Yi Chou Health	Jia Zi Travel	Ji Hai Friends

The "3 Triangle and 4 Middle" (三方四正) is not only limited to the Self, Wealth, Career & Travel Palaces, but can also be applied to any other palaces. However, this is rarely used in the Si Hua Flying Star type of Zi Wei Dou Shu. It is primarily used in the San He method of Zi Wei Dou Shu.

Below is the detailed description of each of the palaces. Do note that all the palaces have both Yin and Yang (阴阳), except for the Self Palace. The explanation for the Yin and Yang is out of the scope of this book, and for more information you can refer to The Fundamentals of Chinese Metaphysics.

Self Palace (命宫)

The Self Palace, or also known as the Life Palace, is equivalent to the Day Master in the Zi Ping Bazi system. It is used as a reference point against the other 11 palaces. This is the only palace that does not have any Yin Yang (阴阳) as it is the reference point.

Stars at Self Palace

Zi Wei (紫微)

People with Zi Wei (紫微) at the Self Palace want to be served like an emperor. As such, they are bossy, stubborn, ambitious, arrogant and likes to go after materialistic things. They like to issue orders and expect others to execute it (just like an emperor).

They like people to suck up to them, which often results in them being manipulated and conned by others.

Wu Qu (武曲)

People with Wu Qu (武曲) at Self Palace are calculative and stingy, and they will not want to spend money on themselves or on others. This would often lead to them being lonely.

Lian Zhen (廉贞)

People with Lian Zhen (廉贞) at Self Palace often feel confined, which makes them highly emotional in nature. Without any reason, they will feel as though they are unable to breathe and would need to take some time alone to clear their minds. In addition, they are stubborn, impatient and temperamental. As such, at times they may do random things that are different from the norm. They will also insist on handling matters alone, and do not want people to help.

However, they are still persistent and diligent people.

Tan Lang (贪狼)

People with Tan Lang (贪狼) at Self Palace are very knowledgeable, and are able to talk about anything. They also have many hobbies However, they have a very unpredictable and volatile temperament. For example, one moment they can be very friendly and the in next moment, they can suddenly be very hostile.

Tan Lang (贪狼) is also a peach blossom star and therefore, people with Tan Lang (贪狼) at Self Palace tends to enjoy the companion of the opposite sex.

Ju Men (巨门)

Ju Men (巨门) represents hiding. For people with Ju Men (巨门) at the Self Palace, they will take a more unconventional career path. For example, they might qualify to be a teacher but choose to become a tutor or tuition teacher instead of a full-time teacher.

Po Jun (破军)

Po Jun (破军) is a destroyer star and therefore, people with Po Jun (破军) at the Self Palace will like to destroy things. This is good if he/she works in the demolition or construction business. Po Jun (破军) people also have a strong personality and are temperamental. Therefore, they might offend others without knowing it. In addition, Po Jun (破军) people have a strong sense of what is right and wrong, and without hesitation, they will be willing to die for a friend.

Tian Ji (天机)

People with Tian Ji (天机) at Self Palace are thinkers, and are smart and intelligent. They are straightforward, which might lead them to offend others.

They have a lot of things going on in their mind, so they will have a lot of things that they would like to do. Therefore, others may see them as fickle or someone who tries to juggle several things at the same time.

Tian Tong (天同)

People with Tian Tong (天同) at Self Palace likes freedom, playing and do not like to take on responsibilities. They will be happy during their childhood but once they reach adulthood, they will be unhappy due to having many responsibilities in life. However, when they retire, they will become happy again as they have none or minimal responsibilities in life.

If they have a sudden inflow of money, the first thing they will do is to spend it and enjoy themselves.

Tian Liang (天梁)

People with Tian Liang (天梁) at Self Palace will not talk much when they are at home. However, they will be very talkative when they go out with good friends.

Tian Liang (天梁) people are eloquent, so they can use this skill to make money. They can have a career in sales or as a motivation speaker.

Although they are very good at talking, they are poor at planning, and this is because they lack self-confidence.

Qi Sha (七杀)

People with Qi Sha (七杀) at Self Palace are courageous, solitary and reserved. They will work hard and will not give up the fight until the end. A such, they are seen as inflexible and stubborn.

Tian Fu (天府)

People with Tian Fu (天府) at Self Palace are stingy and will not want to spend money. In addition, they also have a fickle personality and will easily change their mind.

Tian Xiang (天相)

People with Tian Xiang (天相) at Self Palace do not have a very strong character. As such, their life would be more stable and have less changes. They will not take risks to improve and develop themselves. They prefer the conventional ways of doing things.

Tai Yang (太阳)

People with Tai Yang (太阳) at Self Palace are warm in nature. They are like the Sun at the sky. They may sometimes overcommit themselves to things and are not able to deliver. Because they are generous, they will easily agree to things that they will regret later.

For a female chart, their character is like a man (tomboy).

Tai Yin (太阴)

People with Tai Yin (太阴) in Self Palace are secretive in nature. They will not disclose anything to people who are not close to them. In addition, because Tai Yin (太阴) also represents darkness, they would prefer to work at night or become a Fengshui or Spiritual Master.

For a female chart, they are very organised, neat and clean. They will get upset if things are not put back in its original place.

Wen Chang (文昌)

People with Wen Chang (文昌) at Self Palace are smart and have high IQ. They have a good memory and are adaptable. They will have a stable life.

Wen Qu (文曲)

People with Wen Qu (文曲) at Self Palace are smart, knowledgeable and adaptable. The person will be good in their studies. Sometimes, they can be romantic as well.

Zuo Fu (左輔)

People with Zuo Fu (左輔) at Self Palace are loyal, honest and sincere. Everyone will respect him/her.

You Bi (右弼)

People with You Bi (右弼) at Self Palace are loyal, honest, sincere and forgiving. They are good at strategizing and will always have a plan when handling matters.

Siblings (兄弟)

The Siblings Palace, in Chinese consists of 2 characters: 兄弟. 兄 (Xiōng) means elder brother(s). It refers to the male sibling(s) that is/are older than you. 弟 (Dì) means younger brother(s). It refers to male sibling(s) that is/are younger than you. So, 兄弟 is the Yin Yang (阴阳) of male siblings. The Siblings Palace represents the older and younger male siblings. Some masters use the Siblings Palace to represent female siblings as well, but the correct palace that represent female siblings is the Spouse Palace. (See Spouse Palace for details) In addition, Sibling Palace also represents mother.

Stars at Siblings Palace

Zi Wei (紫微)

People with Zi Wei (紫微) star at Siblings Palace will have authoritative siblings. As the Siblings Palace also represents the mother, the mother of people with Zi Wei star at Siblings Palace will be very authoritative as well.

Wu Qu (武曲)

People with Wu Qu (武曲) star at Siblings Palace will be lonely as their relationship with their siblings will be bad. All of the siblings will not talk to each other.

Lian Zhen (廉贞)

People with Lian Zhen (廉贞) star at Siblings Palace will have a volatile relationship with their siblings. Sometimes, their relationship will be good, and sometimes it will be bad. But in general, it will be mostly bad.

Tan Lang (贪狼)

People with Tan Lang (贪狼) star at Siblings Palace will have a calculative relationship with their siblings. If they ask their sibling for a favour, he/she will first want to know what he/she will get in return for helping you.

People with Tan Lang star at Siblings Palace will most likely have 3 siblings.

Ju Men (巨门)

People with Ju Men (巨门) star at Siblings Palace will always argue with their siblings. Their siblings will not help them when they are in trouble.

Po Jun (破军)

People with Po Jun (破军) star at Siblings Palace will have bad affinity with their siblings. It is not easy for them to work together with their siblings.

Tian Ji (天机)

People with Tian Ji (天机) star at Siblings Palace will have at most 2 siblings, and one of the them will be very successful in academic research.

Tian Tong (天同)

People with Tian Tong (天同) star at Siblings Palace, will have siblings that have a child-like character. Their relationship with their siblings is good, and their siblings will help them when they are in trouble.

Tian Liang (天梁)

People with Tian Liang (天梁) star at Siblings Palace will most likely have a huge age gap with their siblings or they are the youngest sibling. If they have less than three brothers, then the relationship between the siblings will be good. If they have more than three brothers, then the relationship between the siblings will be bad.

Qi Sha (七杀)

People with Qi Sha (七杀) star at Siblings Palace will not have many siblings, and they will not be close to their siblings.

Tian Fu (天府)

People with Tian Fu (天府) star at Siblings Palace will have siblings that are generous and good at socializing. Their siblings are presentable and will dress up to the occasion.

Tian Xiang (天相)

People with Tian Xiang (天相) star at Siblings Palace will not have a close relationship with their siblings.

Tai Yang (太阳)

People with Tai Yang (太阳) star at Sibling Palace will have a close relationship with their siblings. In addition, they will have many brothers.

Tai Yin (太阴)

People with Tai Yin (太阴) star at Sibling Palace will have a good relationship between themselves (for females) and their sisters. The relationship between themselves (for males) and their brothers will not be good as the brothers will like to organise and keep things in a neat and clean manner, which might clash with the person's potentially messy nature.

Wen Chang (文昌)

People with Wen Chang (文昌) star at Sibling Palace will have siblings that are well-known for their talents in literature. They can bring harmony to the family. The relationship between the siblings will be good and they will support and help each other.

Wen Qu (文曲)

People with Wen Qu (文曲) star at Sibling Palace will have a harmonious and happy relationship with their siblings or their friends. This is because they are able to accommodate the thoughts and ideas of others, and they will help you when you are in need.

Zuo Fu (左輔)

People with Zuo Fu (左輔) star at Sibling Palace will have siblings that are smarter than them. Their relationship with their siblings will be good as they will help each other in times of need.

You Bi (右弼)

People with You Bi (右弼) star at Sibling Palace will have a good relationship with their siblings as they will help each other in times of need. In addition, their siblings will be high achievers.

Spouse (夫妻)

The Spouse Palace in Chinese consists of 2 characters -夫妻, which means husband and wife. The Spouse Palace indicates the relationship between you and your significant other. For those who are not married, it also indicates the type of person that you are attracted to. The Spouse Palace also refers to female siblings.

夫 (Fū) – Husband, 妻 (Qī) – Wife. They represent the Yin Yang of Spouse.

Stars at Spouse Palace

Zi Wei (紫微)

People with Zi Wei (紫微) star at Spouse Palace will like someone who is high- class or someone who likes to dress up. In addition, the Spouse's character will be strong, authoritative, responsible, sceptical and emotional.

Wu Qu (武曲)

People with Wu Qu (武曲) star at Spouse Palace will have problems finding a partner and will be lonely. This is because the person views money to be more important than relationships and would not want to spend a lot of time nurturing his/her relationships.

The character of the spouse will be very strong and he/she will be very good in his/her career. The relationship between the husband and the wife will have a lot of ups and down.

Lian Zhen (廉贞)

People with Lian Zhen (廉贞) star at Spouse Palace will have a very exciting and colourful courtship that is full of surprises. However, after marriage, the communication between the husband and the wife will not be very good, and there might be moments where the couple might not speak to each other.

Tan Lang (贪狼)

People with Tan Lang (贪狼) star at Spouse Palace will have a multi-talented spouse that likes partying and having fun. This might lead to relationship problems between the husband and the wife.

Ju Men (巨门)

People with Ju Men (巨门) star at Spouse Palace will secretly admire their potential spouse and will not dare to make a move. They would need to get over their shyness in order to get a spouse. In most cases, they will marry a foreigner or someone from a different dialect group. There will be a lot of arguments between the husband and the wife and his/her spouse will always win the argument.

Po Jun (破军)

People with Po Jun (破军) star at Spouse Palace will have many romantic relationships before finally settling down and getting married. There is also possibility of the person getting married very young, and divorcing before remarrying the same person again. In addition, there is possibility of cohabitation before getting married. As such, it is advisable for the person to marry late.

Tian Ji (天机)

People with Tian Ji (天机) star at Spouse Palace will marry late. However, there will always be arguments between the husband and the wife. For the female chart, they will find a man is successful academically. Also, the older the man, the better it is for her.

Tian Tong (天同)

People with Tian Tong (天同) star at Spouse Palace will have a spouse with a child- like personality or they will like someone that is younger than them.

For the female chart, she will marry someone who is gentle, and they will have a loving relationship. For the male chart, it is better for him to marry late and to marry someone much younger.

Tian Liang (天梁)

For males with Tian Liang (天梁) star at the Spouse Palace, his wife will be older than him. All matters at home will be controlled by his wife. For the female chart, she will have an age difference of 7 years with her husband- either 7 years younger or older.

Qi Sha (七杀)

People with Qi Sha (七杀) star at Spouse Palace will have a bad relationship with their spouse as their spouse will be temperamental. There is also a possibility that both husband and wife might live apart. It is advisable for them to marry late.

Tian Fu (天府)

People with Tian Fu (天府) star at Spouse Palace will have a good relationship with their spouse. The spouse will be capable, strong and good at managing money. Things at home must be organised and set properly and neatly.

Tian Xiang (天相)

People with Tian Xiang (天相) star at Spouse Palace will have an age difference with their spouse that is less than 2 years. Their spouse could be an ex-colleague, ex-school mate, someone that stays in the same area as you (e.g. neighbour) or someone that is from the same dialect group.

Their spouse will have a good temperament, is introverted, kind and does not like to talk much. In addition, the spouse will be good at money management, but his/her health will not be so good.

Tai Yang (太阳)

People with Tai Yang (太阳) star at Spouse Palace will have a spouse whose family is wealthier than theirs. There is possibility that when you are getting married, you will not be able to see your spouse's father or your spouse's mother might have married twice, or your spouse has a god-father.

For the female chart, she will want her husband to be manly. For the male chart, he would like his wife to have the characteristics of a tomboy.

Tai Yin (太阴)

People with Tai Yin (太阴) star at Spouse Palace will have a spouse that will leave the place where he/she was born, or the spouse will not have affinity with his/ her parents/siblings.

For the female chart, her husband might have 2 mothers or a god mother or her husband's father might have a mistress. For the male chart, his wife will want everything to be neat and organised, or alternatively, the person will want a wife who will keep everything neat and organised.

Wen Chang (文昌)

People with Wen Chang (文昌) star at Spouse Palace can easily attract people of the opposite sex. This is not just about looks but people of the opposite sex are just drawn to them and will show affection to them. For the male chart, he will have more affinity with females that are much younger than him. For the female chart, she will have a husband that is intelligent and bright.

Wen Qu (文曲)

People with Wen Qu (文曲) star at Spouse Palace are more sensitive in their relationships. They will easily fall in love at first sight.

Zuo Fu (左輔)

People with Zuo Fu (左輔) star at Spouse Palace will have an unrealistic attitude towards their relationships. They will do some crazy things to win the heart of their partner.

You Bi (右弼)

People with You Bi (右弼) star at Spouse Palace like a very lively type of relationship. Once the relationship becomes stable, they might lose interest and look for new one.

Children (子女)

The Children Palace represents offspring. It also represents someone that is of a lower hierarchy status than you (E.g. your subordinate).

子 – Son, 女 – daughter. They represent the Yin Yang of Children.

Stars at Children Palace

Zi Wei (紫微)

People with Zi Wei (紫微) star at Children Palace will have children with an outstanding and strong character. In addition, the person is not suitable to manage people as he/she will be bullied by his/her staff.

Wu Qu (武曲)

People with Wu Qu (武曲) star at Children Palace, will not have many children. In addition, his/her children's personality will be strong and stubborn. As such, the relationship between the person and his/her children will not be good.

Lian Zhen (廉贞)

People with Lian Zhen (廉贞) star at Children Palace will have difficulty conceiving children. If they have children, their children will be conceived by in- vitro fertilisation (IVF) or born via caesarean.

In addition, their children will have a strong character and will always get into trouble at school. The children would also be closer to their friends than their parents.

Tan Lang (贪狼)

People with Tan Lang (贪狼) star at Children Palace will have children that would rather play than study. In addition, their children would be determined to get the things that they want. The person will also emphasise a lot on his/her children's education and will not hesitate to spend a lot of money in his/her children's tuition.

Ju Men (巨门)

People with Ju Men (巨门) star at Children Palace will encounter some obstacles when trying to have children. The person would need to go through several processes (e.g. operation or medication) in order to have children. However, the children will be eloquent and have good communication skills.

Po Jun (破军)

People with Po Jun (破军) star at Children Palace should have a daughter as the first child. Otherwise, if it is male, then there is chance of miscarriage. Their daughters will have good achievements, whereas the sons will struggle. In general, the children do not like staying at home.

Tian Ji (天机)

People with Tian Ji (天机) star at Children Palace will have at most 2 children. Their children would be cunning, scheming and street-smart. They would also like to move about and cannot sit still. They are likely to change teachers often. In addition, their children are likely to be born by caesarean or there might be a complicated birth process.

Tian Tong (天同)

People with Tian Tong (天同) star at Children Palace will have children that are playful and do not like to study.

Tian Liang (天梁)

For people with Tian Liang (天梁) star at Children Palace, if they are trying for a son, they will have to wait until they are old in order to get a son. Their children will be bright and intelligent and likes technology and studying.

Qi Sha (七杀)

People with Qi Sha (七杀) star at Children Palace will have children with a strong character. Their children will always have clashing opinions with them. In addition, there is also chance of miscarriage.

Tian Fu (天府)

People with Tian Fu (天府) star at Children Palace will have children who are intelligent, agile and bright. They will be known for their talents and bring honour to the family.

Tian Xiang (天相)

People with Tian Xiang (天相) star at Children Palace they will provide basic necessities for their children and give minimal care but will not give their full attention. Their children will like to eat and hence will put on weight. Their children will be honest and may not like to play with other children.

Tai Yang (太阳)

People with Tai Yang (太阳) star at Children Palace will have children with a lot of achievements. If Tai Yang (太阳) star is at Hai Palace, the person would have a lot of children, but all of them will be of the same sex. Their children will be active and full of energy, and the type that would love sports

Tai Yin (太阴)

For people with Tai Yin (太阴) star at Children Palace, if the first born is male, then the rest of the children will be male. If the first born is female, then the rest of the children will be female.

Their children will be talented and educated. They will have a special talent in literature or art.

Wen Chang (文昌)

People with Wen Chang (文昌) star at Children Palace will have extraverted children. Their children will look demure and elegant. At an old age, they will be able to get support from their children and be able to enjoy life to the fullest.

Wen Qu (文曲)

People with Wen Qu (文曲) star at Children Palace will have a good relationship with their children. Their children will be well behaved and will know how to make their parents happy. When their children grow up, they will become famous.

Zuo Fu (左辅)

People with Zuo Fu (左辅) star at Children Palace, will not need to worry about their children. Their children will know how to take care of themselves and will not give their parents any trouble.

You Bi (右弼)

People with You Bi (右弼) star at Children Palace will have bright and intelligent children. They will take care of the household and help out around the house, especially the daughters.

Wealth (財帛)

The Chinese meaning of Wealth Palace is 財帛. 財 (Cái) means Money. 帛 (Bó) means Silk. The actual meaning of Wealth Palace is rewards; or things that people give you for your effort. In ancient China, people could be paid in gold/silver ingots or silk. For example, in ancient China, generals will be awarded with rewards such as gold/silver ingots, silk, house as well as land after winning a war. So, gold/silver ingots are the 財 (Cái) aspect, and silk is the 帛 (Bó) aspect of the Wealth Palace.

Please note that 財 (Cái) is different from 祿 (Lù) (see Career Palace for more details)

House and Land is considered under the Property Palace. Therefore, to see a person's wealth, we also look at the Property Palace.

Stars at Wealth Palace

Zi Wei (紫微)

People with Zi Wei (紫微) star at Wealth Palace likes to keep antiques or similar valuable things. They will have several different types of assets and apart from keeping currencies from various countries, they will also like to keep gold, jewellery, land etc.

Wu Qu (武曲)

People with Wu Qu (武曲) star at Wealth Palace will need to put in a lot of effort to make money.

Lian Zhen (廉贞)

People with Lian Zhen (廉贞) star at Wealth Palace will always feel like they are always short of money, even if they are wealthy in other people's standard. Sometimes, their cash flow is not smooth, but that is only temporary. Therefore, they will need to have good money management.

The process of making money will not be easy for them and there will be a lot of ups and downs.

Tan Lang (贪狼)

People with Tan Lang (贪狼) star at Wealth Palace likes to spend money mainly on entertainment and enjoyment. To maximise their wealth luck, it is advisable for them to be involved in the education and entertainment sector. They will be successful in the things that they like and enjoy, as they will have a strong desire to achieve results.

Ju Men (巨门)

People with Ju Men (巨门) star at Wealth Palace will earn money from the type of work that requires arguing or debating. They could be seminar speakers or lawyers.

Po Jun (破军)

People with Po Jun (破军) star at Wealth Palace will need to fail first before they can succeed. Therefore, they will not be able to get rich early (before 32 years old) as they will most likely fail. However, if they do get rich before 32 years old and fail, they will become even more successful after that.

Tian Ji (天机)

People with Tian Ji (天机) star at Wealth Palace will have an unstable income, but are not necessarily poor. They will worry about their wealth for their whole life. They will think a lot before spending as they are fickle-minded. They have to work very hard to earn money.

Tian Tong (天同)

People with Tian Tong (天同) star at Wealth Palace make money from professions that are related to children (e.g. kindergarten). The person's wealth luck is smooth and minimum effort is required for him/her to gain wealth. They also like to keep antiques.

Tian Liang (天梁)

People with Tian Liang (天梁) star at Wealth Palace can inherit other people's asset. That means that they are able to benefit from other people. Most of the time, they make money from the public sector or in a business related to the government.

Qi Sha (七杀)

People with Qi Sha (七杀) star at Wealth Palace will have a decent wealth luck, but money will come and go easily. They can be rich in the morning and poor at night. So, their wealth is unstable and will always have ups and downs.

Tian Fu (天府)

People with Tian Fu (天府) star at Wealth Palace will need to get into businesses related to basic necessities in order to be successful.

Tian Xiang (天相)

People with Tian Xiang (天相) star at Wealth Palace will have a good wealth luck if they are working as a secretary, admin staff, head-hunter, middleman or tour agent.

Tai Yang (太阳)

People with Tai Yang (太阳) star at Wealth Palace are generous when spending their money. They can also earn money from very competitive ways such as share investment. They can also earn money from a job that requires a highly specialised skill. They also have good money management skills.

Tai Yin (太阴)

People with Tai Yin (太阴) star at Wealth Palace will buy property when they have money, and will always invest in property.

If they are born in Ding Year and Tai Yin (太阴) is at the Property Palace, the person will have a lot of properties.

Wen Chang (文昌)

People with Wen Chang (文昌) star at Wealth Palace, they will not have to worry about basic necessities for their entire life.

Wen Qu (文曲)

For people with Wen Qu (文曲) star at Wealth Palace, when they have wealth, status and reputation will come with it. They are very good in financial management and have good personal opinions on matters regarding investment.

Zuo Fu (左辅)

People with Zuo Fu (左辅) star at Wealth Palace will not have to worry about the basic necessities for their whole life. Although they need to work hard, they will always have enough to eat.

You Bi (右弼)

People with You Bi (右弼) star at Wealth Palace will not have to worry about the basic necessities for their whole life. They will not be satisfied with just one type of career, and will want to try different types of careers.

Health (疾厄)

The Chinese character for Health Palace is 疾厄 (Jí è). 疾 (Jí) means fast, quick and a painful type of illness. 厄 (è) means slow, dormant and inherited type of illness.

Together, they represent the health condition of the person.

Stars at Health Palace

Zi Wei (紫微)

People with Zi Wei (紫微) star at Health Palace will have problems with his/her spleen and stomach. They will like to eat good and expensive food, which might be bad for health.

Wu Qu (武曲)

People with Wu Qu (武曲) star at Health Palace will have problems related to his/her lung and big intestine.

Lian Zhen (廉贞)

People with Lian Zhen (廉贞) star at Health Palace will have problems with their heart, or will have tumour or illnesses that are not easily cured.

Tan Lang (贪狼)

People with Tan Lang (贪狼) star at Health Palace will suffer from sex related illnesses or illnesses related to the gallbladder.

Ju Men (巨门)

People with Ju Men (巨门) star at Health Palace will suffer from problems with their urinal track.

Po Jun (破军)

People with Po Jun (破军) star at Health Palace will generally have a high chance of getting diabetes. For both the male and the female charts, they might have genital- related problems or illness.

Tian Ji (天机)

People with Tian Ji (天机) star at Health Palace will probably wear glasses since young. For the male chart, there is possibility that he may have problems with his prostate. For the female chart, there is possibility that she may have problems with her womb.

Tian Tong (天同)

People with Tian Tong (天同) star at Health Palace may have water retention problems or problems with their kidney and/or bladder.

Tian Liang (天梁)

People with Tian Liang (天梁) star at Health Palace will probably have problems related to the stomach.

Qi Sha (七杀)

People with Qi Sha (七杀) star at Health Palace might be sick ever since they were young. In addition, they might have problems with their respiratory track.

Tian Fu (天府)

People with Tian Fu (天府) star at Health Palace will have problems with their stomach due to eating too much good food.

Tian Xiang (天相)

People with Tian Xiang (天相) star at Health Palace will have urinal track infection or skin problems.

Tai Yang (太阳)

People with Tai Yang (太阳) star at Health Palace will have illness related to the heart or eyes (myopia). In addition, they will have illness related to head and may frequently experience headaches or giddiness. In addition, there is possibility that they will have high blood pressure.

Tai Yin (太阴)

People with Tai Yin (太阴) star at Health Palace may have problems with their bladder. In addition, they may have eczema or diabetes.

Wen Chang (文昌)

People with Wen Chang (文昌) star at Health Palace will not have many problems with their health. Their weak organs are the intestines, lungs and ears.

Wen Qu (文曲)

People with Wen Qu (文曲) star at Health Palace will not have many problems with their health. Their weak organs are the gallbladder and liver. In addition, they might have freckles or rough skin.

Zuo Fu (左輔)

People with Zuo Fu (左輔) star at Health Palace will not have any major sickness or illness. Their weak organs are the spleen and the stomach.

You Bi (右弼)

People with You Bi (右弼) star at Health Palace will not have many problems with their health. However, their weak organ is the mouth. This means that it will be easy for the person to get sore throats and dry mouth.

Travel (遷移)

遷移 (Qiān Yí) comes from the word 搬遷 (Bān Qiān) and 移动 (Yí Dòng). In ancient China, people do not normally move out of their village. If they do, they will organize a ceremony before the person moves out. So, 搬遷 (Bān Qiān) means to move out far away from village, while (Yí Dòng) is to move from one house to another house within the village. Looking at this in a modern context, 搬遷 (Bān Qiān) represents going far away (e.g. migration or going overseas) and 移动 (Yí Dòng) represents traveling from one location to another.

Therefore, Travel Palace represents migration, moving house, going on tour as well as modes of transport.

Stars at Travel Palace

Zi Wei (紫微)

People with Zi Wei (紫微) star at Travel Palace will spend a lot of money when travelling. They will not go alone and will always need someone to accompany them. In addition, when travelling, there will be noblemen coming to help them, especially elders.

Wu Qu (武曲)

People with Wu Qu (武曲) star at Travel Palace will have a lot of opportunities to work overseas. In addition, when travelling, they will come across several opportunities that they can take advantage of. For example, they may go on a holiday tour and meet someone who might later hire him/her.

Lian Zhen (廉贞)

People with Lian Zhen (廉贞) star at Travel Palace will encounter a lot of delays when they go overseas. There will be a lot of obstacles if they plan to migrate. However, when they travel, they will have more affinity with the opposite sex. Working overseas or moving house often will bring them better opportunities in life.

Tan Lang (贪狼)

People with Tan Lang (贪狼) star at Travel Palace will truly enjoy themselves when they travel. They will indulge themselves with good food and drinks.

Ju Men (巨门)

People with Ju Men (巨门) star at Travel Palace will lose their things easily and are likely to encounter theft.

Po Jun (破军)

People with Po Jun (破军) star at Travel Palace will have a lot of obstacles if they want to travel or move house. They will feel miserable if they work overseas.

Tian Ji (天机)

People with Tian Ji (天机) star at Travel Palace will have a high chance of getting into accidents when overseas.

Tian Tong (天同)

People with Tian Tong (天同) star at Travel Palace will be able to enjoy and have fun when they go on tour or work overseas. There will be people driving them around and bringing them out to enjoy good food. In addition, noblemen will always come to help them when they are overseas.

Tian Liang (天梁)

People with Tian Liang (天梁) star at Travel Palace will not encounter any problems when travelling. If they lose anything, they will be able to get it back.

Qi Sha (七杀)

People with Qi Sha (七杀) star at Travel Palace will have a higher chance of getting into accidents when overseas.

Tian Fu (天府)

People with Tian Fu (天府) star at Travel Palace, will be able to travel comfortably when they go overseas. In addition, noblemen will always come to help them when they encounter problems.

Tian Xiang (天相)

People with Tian Xiang (天相) star at Travel Palace prefers travelling with a wide variety of friends. They may also meet a wide variety of friends while travelling.

Tai Yang (太阳)

People with Tai Yang (太阳) star at Travel Palace will go to places with a lot of people when they travel/ go on a tour. In addition, there is possibility that they will leave home when young, or that they will grow up at someone else's house. They also do not like to stay at home and will always want to go out.

Tai Yin (太阴)

People with Tai Yin (太阴) star at Travel Palace will have a higher chance of getting into accidents when they travel. However, they are able to get help from others, especially from female friends.

Wen Chang (文昌)

People with Wen Chang (文昌) star at Travel Palace will have a smooth life if they work overseas.

Wen Qu (文曲)

People with Wen Qu (文曲) star at Travel Palace, will always have noblemen coming to help them. If they seek wealth, they will get wealth.

Zuo Fu (左辅)

People with Zuo Fu (左辅) star at Travel Palace will always have noblemen coming to help them.

You Bi (右弼)

People with You Bi (右弼) star at Travel Palace are able to achieve things due to the help of noblemen.

Friends (交友)

The Chinese word for the Friends Palace is 交友 (Jiāo Yǒu). 交 (Jiāo) refers to acquaintances, which are people you might know but are not close to. 友(Yǒu) means friends or people you are close to.

Stars at Friends Palace

Zi Wei (紫微)

People with Zi Wei (紫微) star at Friends Palace will have a lot of friends that are very capable, and most of their friends will be more capable than them.

Wu Qu (武曲)

People with Wu Qu (武曲) star at Friends Palace will have a lot of friends, but some of their friends will get them in trouble.

Lian Zhen (廉贞)

People with Lian Zhen (廉贞) star at Friends Palace will have difficulties finding good friends. They will have more friends that are of the opposite sex than friends of the same sex.

Tan Lang (贪狼)

People with Tan Lang (贪狼) star at Friends Palace will meet their friends through parties, entertainment or social gatherings. They will have friends that enjoys partying and having fun.

Ju Men (巨门)

People with Ju Men (巨门) star at Friends Palace will often have misunderstandings between them and their friends. In addition, they will have problems controlling their subordinates.

Po Jun (破军)

People with Po Jun (破军) star at Friends Palace will have friends that are of different backgrounds. In addition, their friends are very capable, and there is chance that they may be sabotaged by their friends.

Tian Ji (天机)

People with Tian Ji (天机) star at Friends Palace will have friends with various talents. In addition, they will keep changing friends.

Tian Tong (天同)

People with Tian Tong (天同) star at Friends Palace will have a good relationship with their friends and their friends will help them a lot. In addition, they will have many friends that enjoys partying and playing.

Tian Liang (天梁)

People with Tian Liang (天梁) star at Friends Palace like to make friends with older people. In addition, the Friends Palace also represents the boss. Thus, the older the boss, the better it is for them.

Qi Sha (七杀)

People with Qi Sha (七杀) star at Friends Palace will have friends that will always like to command them to do things. These friends will always give them trouble and they will have to resolve the issue for their friends. For them, it is better to have less friends.

Tian Fu (天府)

People with Tian Fu (天府) star at Friends Palace will have a lot of friends that are from a good family background. Their friends will be willing to help them when needed.

Tian Xiang (天相)

People with Tian Xiang (天相) star at Friends Palace usually make friends with the same type of people and their friends are usually quite average, i.e, friends that do not have outstanding achievements. Their friends are more like close acquaintances rather than real friends.

Tai Yang (太阳)

People with Tai Yang (太阳) star at Friends Palace will have all sorts of friends (good and bad) and their friends will come from various family backgrounds.

Tai Yin (太阴)

People with Tai Yin (太阴) star at Friends Palace will have more affinity with female friends. This is applicable to both the male and the female chart

Wen Chang (文昌)

People with Wen Chang (文昌) star at Friends Palace likes to make friends with intellectual people. All their friends will have a high status and good reputation. If they are a supervisor in a company, they will have capable employees that are able to help them in their career advancement.

Wen Qu (文曲)

People with Wen Qu (文曲) star at Friends Palace, their friends are people that they rely on when they run into problems. They should listen to the opinions of their friends as it will help them with their endeavours.

Zuo Fu (左輔)

People with Zuo Fu (左輔) star at Friends Palace will make money with the help of their friends.

You Bi (右弼)

People with You Bi (右弼) star at Friends Palace are able to have achievements due to the help of their friends. However, such help will not be money- related.

Career (官祿)

In ancient China, a person is considered successful in his career when he (women did not work in the past) passes his exam and holds an official post in the government. There are 9 levels of minster or 官 (Guān); where the first and highest level is the Prime Minister. So, when a person holds a position in the government, the person will be paid based on their position level and this payment is called 祿 (Lù). So, 官祿 (Guān Lù) is the official position and the salary or remuneration you receive based on the position.

So, a person with a good Career will have good remuneration, and if he/she invest or save correctly, he/she will be able to have wealth.

Stars at Career Palace

Zi Wei (紫微)

People with Zi Wei (紫微) star at Career Palace are suitable for a career that requires high precision or a career related to jewellery (e.g. watch making, jeweller etc).

Wu Qu (武曲)

People with Wu Qu (武曲) star at Career Palace are suitable for a career related to finance.

Lian Zhen (廉贞)

People with Lian Zhen (廉贞) star at Career Palace are very patient in their work and are therefore suitable for a career that requires craftsmanship. It is also good for them to be civil servants or teachers.

Tan Lang (贪狼)

People with Tan Lang (贪狼) star at Career Palace are suitable to be in the food and beverage, education or entertainment- related industry. Examples of entertainment- related careers include modelling, acting, karaoke hostess etc. They have an entrepreneur type of mindset.

Ju Men (巨门)

People with Ju Men (巨门) star at Career Palace are suitable for a career that requires them to talk a lot. They are suitable to be professors, teachers, lawyers, politicians, motivation speakers etc.

Po Jun (破军)

People with Po Jun (破军) star at Career Palace are suitable for a career in the renovation and demolition industry. They are also suitable to be in the public security sector. An example of a career in the public security sector is a prison officer. For any other businesses, they will need to have a one-time failure before it can be successful. Furthermore, when they are young, their career will not be smooth.

Tian Ji (天机)

People with Tian Ji (天机) star at Career Palace are advised to go into a career that requires them to move around or a career that is based on commissions as Tian Ji (天机) represents movement. Examples of jobs/industries include marketing, sales, agents etc. If their job does not require them to move around, then there will be a lot of changes in their career and their career will not be stable.

Tian Tong (天同)

People with Tian Tong (天同) star at Career Palace do not have a mindset of an entrepreneur and are thus not suitable to start their own business. In addition, they are the type that cannot sit still in the office for the whole day and would need to move about. As such, a sales or freelance career would be suitable for them.

Tian Liang (天梁)

People with Tian Liang (天梁) star at Career Palace are suitable to be in the industry that requires them to take care of people. For example, they can work in childcare centres, old folk's home, nursing home etc. Alternatively, they can pursue a consulting career.

Qi Sha (七杀)

People with Qi Sha (七杀) star at Career Palace are suitable for a career that is physical challenging. Examples include a professional athlete, police officer or army officer.

Tian Fu (天府)

People with Tian Fu (天府) star at Career Palace are suitable for a career involving property or a career related to basic necessities. For example, they can be a property sales person, property developer or a mini mart owner.

Tian Xiang (天相)

People with Tian Xiang (天相) star at Career Palace are suitable to be in a career that does not have many changes. For example, they can do back-end processing or day-to-day administrative type of work.

Tai Yang (太阳)

People with Tai Yang (太阳) star at Career Palace will need to get into a career that requires them to compete with others in order to be successful. In order for them to get recognition, they will need to work hard and fight for it to gain the respect of others. For example, a professional athlete will need to win competitions to gain the recognition of others. For employees, they will need to work very hard to gain recognition from their boss in order to be promoted and successful.

They can have careers or businesses that are short-term, i.e, they can work jobs that last for a few months or open their business for a few months.

Tai Yin (太阴)

People with Tai Yin (太阴) star at Career Palace are suitable to be in the property or female- related (e.g. manicure, make-up, salon) industry. They can also do jobs that are related to Fengshui, or jobs that requires them to work at night (e.g. night shift worker).

Wen Chang (文昌)

People with Wen Chang (文昌) star at Career Palace are good at literature and art. As such, they will have significant achievements if their career is related to literature and/or art. They are also suitable for jobs related to literature, the arts, design, music composing or anything that requires creativity.

Wen Qu (文曲)

People with Wen Qu (文曲) star at Career Palace are good at writing. As such, they are suitable to be in a career related to writing (E.g Author) or news reporting.

Zuo Fu (左輔)

People with Zuo Fu (左輔) star at Career Palace are good at planning and execution. As such, they suitable for a career in project planning and management.

You Bi (右弼)

People with You Bi (右弼) star at Career Palace approach their tasks in a calm and non-aggressive manner. They will also approach conflicts with a mediation mindset. This might result in them having to do more work as they will not take the aggressive, straightforward approach in completing their work, which might be the more efficient approach.

Property (田宅)

The Chinese word for Property Palace is 田宅 (Tián Zhái). 田 (Tián) means field or farmland. 宅 (Zhái) means house. So, together it means farmland and house. In modern context, Property Palace represent tangible asset such as property or fixed savings in the bank.

Stars at Property Palace

Zi Wei (紫微)

People with Zi Wei (紫微) star at Property Palace likes to stay on higher floors or places that are on high terrains. They also like big or expensive properties.

Wu Qu (武曲)

People with Wu Qu (武曲) star at Property Palace are likely to stay near places that have large buildings, buildings that are cylindrical in shape or financial institutes.

Lian Zhen (廉贞)

People with Lian Zhen (廉贞) star at Property Palace are likely to stay near things that are colourful (e.g. traffic light). Also, the electronic appliances in their house will spoil easily. They would often stress about matters of the house matter as well as worry about moving house. If the person is running their ancestor's business, it will not be successful.

Tan Lang (贪狼)

People with Tan Lang (贪狼) star at Property Palace are not suitable to invest in property. They need to be careful as there may be uncertainties regarding the transaction and purchase of the property.

If they really need/want to purchase properties, they have to be extra careful and engage someone that they can trust to help out.

Ju Men (巨门)

People with Ju Men (巨门) star at Property Palace are likely to stay near a graveyard or a Yin temple. In addition, they will not take over their ancestor's business if there is any.

Po Jun (破军)

People with Po Jun (破军) star at Property Palace are likely to stay near a market or a place that is disorganised. They may encounter a lot of problems if they purchase a brand new house. As such, it is advisable for them to purchase a 2nd hand house. In addition, they tend to change house frequently.

Tian Ji (天机)

People with Tian Ji (天机) star at Property Palace, they like to change house. They will not be able to fully utilise their ancestor's property to their advantage.

Tian Tong (天同)

People with Tian Tong (天同) star at Property Palace are likely to stay near the places where there is a swimming pool or places where there are a lot of children.

Tian Liang (天梁)

People with Tian Liang (天梁) star at Property Palace are likely to stay near an old folks' home. Alternatively, they may not own any property.

Qi Sha (七杀)

People with Qi Sha (七杀) star at Property Palace, are likely to stay at/own properties that will be acquired by others.

Tian Fu (天府)

People with Tian Fu (天府) star at Property Palace are likely to stay in a decent and complete house. They could be staying at a high-end property or a place that is near a bank. They will also have a lot of snacks available at home.

Tian Xiang (天相)

People with Tian Xiang (天相) star at Property Palace will have stability in the properties that they own. If they work hard, they will be able to accumulate more properties.

Tai Yang (太阳)

People with Tai Yang (太阳) star at Property Palace are likely to stay near a church or a mosque. If they own property from their ancestors, they will need to further develop the property or else it will be lost.

Tai Yin (太阴)

People with Tai Yin (太阴) star at Property Palace are likely to stay near the forest or the park. They are suitable to own farm(s) or deal with goods related to flower or plants. The property that they own might be inherited from their parents.

Wen Chang (文昌)

People with Wen Chang (文昌) star at Property Palace will have to slog and work very hard for their wealth and to own/rent their property during the early stages of their life, but they will be able to reap the benefits when old.

Wen Qu (文曲)

People with Wen Qu (文曲) star at Property Palace are likely to inherit their ancestor's business and make it even more successful.

Zuo Fu (左輔)

People with Zuo Fu (左輔) star at Property Palace will have to work hard to gain success. They will also inherit their ancestor's business.

You Bi (右弼)

People with You Bi (右弼) star at Property Palace will be able to successfully start their own business. However, there has to be another auspicious star to be together with the You Bi (右弼) star at Property Palace for this to happen.

Mental (福德)

福 (Fú) means good fortune, blessing and happiness. From the spiritual or religious perspective, it is your karma merit due to the good things that you have done in your previous life, or the good things your ancestors did before you were born. 德 (Dé) means virtue or morals. From the spiritual or religious perspective, based on the 福 (Fú) karma merit that you have, you will get the equivalent 德 (Dé) virtue. In other words, it is the Cause and Effect of karma system.

To put this in a non-religious context, the Mental Palace represents your inner thinking and your spiritual wellbeing.

Stars at Mental Palace

Zi Wei (紫微)

People with Zi Wei (紫微) star at Mental Palace are lonely because of their pride, and they do not know how to express themselves.

Wu Qu (武曲)

People with Wu Qu (武曲) star at Mental Palace are likely to have a difficult and tiring life. They know how to make money but do not know how to enjoy their wealth.

Lian Zhen (廉贞)

People with Lian Zhen (廉贞) star at Mental Palace are likely to have fluctuating emotions. In addition, they enjoy being busy with work and are likely to be workaholics.

Tan Lang (贪狼)

People with Tan Lang (贪狼) star at Mental Palace likes to party and enjoy themselves. They have gourmet's luck (i.e they will always be able to eat good food) and they like to enjoy good food.

Ju Men (巨门)

People with Ju Men (巨门) star at Mental Palace are always stressed and may have the intention to commit suicide.

Po Jun (破军)

People with Po Jun (破军) star at Mental Palace, they will work very hard but are unable to produce results. Because of this, they are constantly stressed and their mind will not be at peace. In addition, they have a high chance of getting into accidents.

Tian Ji (天机)

People with Tian Ji (天机) star at Mental Palace are likely to have depression and anxiety issues.

Tian Tong (天同)

People with Tian Tong (天同) star at Mental Palace are always happy and will not have many mental issues or problems. Even if there is a problem, they are able to let go and carry on.

Tian Liang (天梁)

People with Tian Liang (天梁) star at Mental Palace likes to talk a lot and will often repeat themselves. Overall, they will have a peaceful life.

Qi Sha (七杀)

People with Qi Sha (七杀) star at Mental Palace are likely to have a busy and hard life as they will only focus on their work. In addition, they demand too much of themselves and will thus become internally drained.

Tian Fu (天府)

People with Tian Fu (天府) star at Mental Palace, might have a bit of Obsessive-compulsive disorder (OCD), i.e, things must be done in a certain way and things must be placed a certain way in order for them to be mentally satisfied.

Tian Xiang (天相)

People with Tian Xiang (天相) star at Mental Palace will want a stable life. They are the type of people that will stay in their comfort zone and do not want to take on additional responsibilities or be promoted.

Tai Yang (太阳)

People with Tai Yang (太阳) star at Mental Palace are constantly stressed. This is because they have high expectations of themselves and want to be seen and look good in public.

Tai Yin (太阴)

People with Tai Yin (太阴) at Mental Palace like to be pretty and will spend a lot of money dolling up. In addition, they like things to be neat and orderly, and they will stress over it. For the males, they are likely to have a comfortable life and they will have good affinity with the females.

Wen Chang (文昌)

People with Wen Chang (文昌) at Mental Palace are likely to have a happy and long life.

Wen Qu (文曲)

People with Wen Qu (文曲) at Mental Palace have very strong analytical skills.

Zuo Fu (左輔)

People with Zuo Fu (左輔) at Mental Palace are quite nosy and they like to go out and socialise with different types of people. They can make use of such skills to be successful in their career.

You Bi (右弼)

People with You Bi (右弼) at Mental Palace are very sociable and compassionate. They are often involved in charity- related activities.

Parents (父母)

父 (Fù) means Father. 母 (Mǔ) means Mother. Both words combine to form the Yin Yang of Parents. The Parents Palace represents both the father and mother in general, as well as a higher authority. However, for more a detailed analysis, the Pare nts Palace can be used to represent the Father, and Siblings Palace can be used to represent the Mother.

Stars at Parents Palace

Zi Wei (紫微)

People with Zi Wei (紫微) star at Parents Palace are likely to have very strict parents. Their parents will have power and status.

Wu Qu (武曲)

People with Wu Qu (武曲) star at Parents Palace are likely to have parents that will not invest in them as their parents will value money to be more important than them.

Lian Zhen (廉贞)

People with Lian Zhen (廉贞) star at Parents Palace are likely to have very strict parents. As the Parents Palace also represents higher authority, people with Lian Zhen (廉贞) star at Parents Palace are likely to get into lawsuits or have legal issues. In addition, they might get a traffic fine for no reason.

Tan Lang (贪狼)

People with Tan Lang (贪狼) star at Parents Palace are likely to have parents that will emphasise a lot on their education and will spend a lot of money on their education and tuition.

Ju Men (巨门)

People with Ju Men (巨门) star at Parents Palace are likely to have insecure parents who will not trust them in most important things.

Po Jun (破军)

People with Po Jun (破军) star at Parents Palace will need to fail in their education first (e.g. repeat, fail to pass or fail to enter college/school) before it becomes good. They might have to leave home when young. In addition, their parents might often have disagreements related to the person.

Tian Ji (天机)

People with Tian Ji (天机) star at Parents Palace will always have movement and changes in their education teachings and methods. This causes them to have difficulties in adjusting which will affect their education.

Tian Tong (天同)

People with Tian Tong (天同) star at Parents Palace are likely to have parents that are very liberal and will not control them much.

Tian Liang (天梁)

People with Tian Liang (天梁) star at Parents Palace are likely to have parents that will live long.

Qi Sha (七杀)

People with Qi Sha (七杀) star at Parents Palace are likely to have stubborn and overbearing parents. When they are young, they might not stay with their parents (E.g. They might be fostered out or they might stay with their grandparents)

Tian Fu (天府)

People with Tian Fu (天府) star at Parents Palace are likely to have parents that will take care of all of their basic necessities. Everything at home will be proper, neat and complete. Their parents will also have good achievements.

Tian Xiang (天相)

People with Tian Xiang (天相) star at Parents Palace are likely to have parents that are liberal or negligent, and will not control them much when they are young. In addition, their parents might be public servants.

Tai Yang (太阳)

People with Tai Yang (太阳) star at Parents Palace are likely to have parents that will give them a lot of problem.

Tai Yin (太阴)

People with Tai Yin (太阴) at Parents Palace are likely to have a father with two wives or they might have a godmother. In addition, their mother might have a lot of illnesses.

Wen Chang (文昌)

People with Wen Chang (文昌) at Parents Palace are likely to have parents that are into literature and art. Therefore, they will be exposed to literature and art when they are young.

Wen Qu (文曲)

People with Wen Qu (文曲) at Parents Palace are likely to have accomplished parents that are very sociable. They will be deeply influenced by their parents' achievements and will want to follow in their parents' footstep.

Zuo Fu (左輔)

People with Zuo Fu (左輔) at Parents Palace will have good relationships with their parents and elders. As such, they will get help from their parents and their elders while growing up.

You Bi (右弼)

People with You Bi (右弼) at Parents Palace are likely to have good relationships with their parents and elders. Therefore, they will get help from their parents and elders while growing up.

Si Hua (四化)

The key to Si Hua lineage of Zi Wei Dou Shu is the Si Hua formula. Si Hua (四化) consists of two words; 四 (Si) means Four in English. 化 (Hua) means to change, transform, convert or influence. Some English book translate Si Hua (四化) as *four transformation* or *four influence*. I prefer to leave it as Si Hua (四化) to retain the actual Chinese meaning.

Si Hua (四化) is based on seasonal information; the season of the Earth when it rotates around the Sun. Si Hua (四化) definition is as follows:

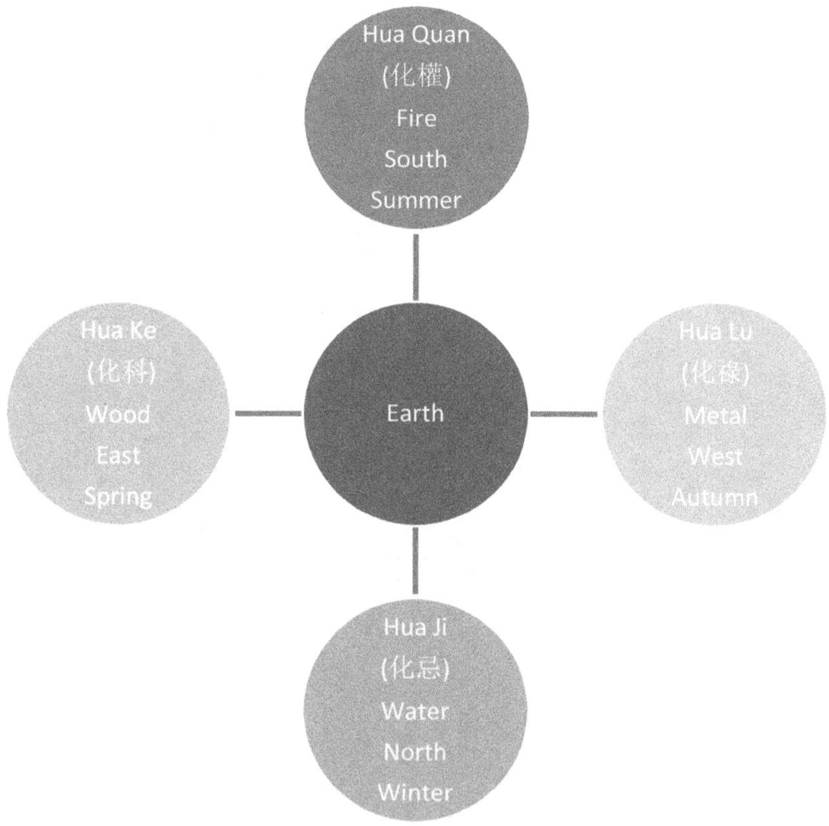

Therefore, the Si Hua (四化) or the four Hua (化) are Hua Ke (化科), Hua Quan (化權), Hua Lu (化祿) and Hua Ji (化忌).

Hua Ke (化科)

Hua (化) means to change, transform, convert or influence. Ke (科) refers to a branch of academic study or a subject. Together, Hua Ke (化科) means *transformation of academic*.

Hua Ke (化科) has the following attributes:

Attribute	Value
Element	Wood
Season	Spring
Direction	East
Meaning	Planning, nobleman

The reason why Hua Ke (化科) means *transformation of academic* is because Hua Ke (化科) is a Wood element. In Chinese Metaphysics, academics are a Wood element.

In the past, China was an agriculture country, and agriculture is dependent on the season. During the spring season, which is usually after Chinese New Year, farmers will start to plan the types of crops that they want to plant so that they can harvest it during autumn. It is like planning for your life, in which you plan what you want to achieve and embark on the study of those subjects.

When studying, there will be a teacher teaching or helping you. As such, Hua Ke (化科) also represents someone coming to help.

Hua Quan (化權)

Hua (化) means to change, transform, convert or influence. Quan (權) also means power or authority. Together Hua Quan (化權) means *transformation of power*.

Hua Quan (化權) has the following attributes:

Attribute	Value
Element	Fire
Season	Summer
Direction	South
Meaning	Power, struggle, scarify

In an agriculture society, summer is the time when the farmer has to work hard under the blazing sun on his/her land.

Therefore, Hua Quan (化權) has the meaning of a power struggle or sacrifice.

Hua Lu (化祿)

Hua (化) means to change, transform, convert or influence. Lu (祿) represents the remuneration from work done (salary). Together, Hua Lu (化祿) means ***transformation remuneration***. It means getting good remuneration for the work done.

Hua Lu (化祿) has the following attributes:

Attribute	Value
Element	Metal
Season	Autumn
Direction	West
Meaning	Harvest, returns, keep/storage.

In an agriculture society, autumn is the time when food is abundant. It is also the time when the harvests are kept in a secure storage. When the harvest is good, there is abundant food for everyone.

Therefore, Hua Lu (化祿) means abundance or good returns.

Hua Ji (化忌)

Hua (化) means to change, transform, convert or influence. Ji (忌) means to resist, fear or dread. Together Hua Ji (化忌) means *transformation of fear*.

Hua Ji (化忌) has the following attributes:

Attribute	Value
Element	Water
Season	Winter
Direction	North
Meaning	Fear, dread, abstain, cold

In an ancient agriculture society, winter is too cold for farming. Therefore, the farmer will have to be prudent with their food. It is also the time when it is cold and there is a lack of food.

Therefore, Hua Ji (化忌) means to abstain.

Stars Si Hua (四化)

Star Si Hua (四化) is the mapping of Heavenly Steam with Zi Wei Dou Shu stars to form the transformation.

Si Hua / Heavenly Stems	Hua Lu (化祿)	Hua Quan (化權)	Hua Ke (化科)	Hua Ji (化忌)
Jia	Lian Zhen	Po Jun	Wu Qu	Tai Yang
Yi	Tian Ji	Tian Liang	Zi Wei	Tai Yin
Bing	Tian Tong	Tian Ji	Wen Chang	Lian Zhen
Ding	Tai Yin	Tian Tong	Tian Ji	Ju Men
Wu	Tan Lang	Tai Yin	You Bi	Tian Ji
Ji	Wu Qu	Tan Lang	Tian Liang	Wen Qu
Geng	Tai Yang	Wu Qu	Tai Yin	Tian Tong
Xin	Ju Men	Tai Yang	Wen Qu	Wen Chang
Ren	Tian Liang	Zi Wei	Zuo Fu	Wu Qu
Gui	Po Jun	Ju Men	Tai Yin	Tan Lang

For example, Jia Heavenly Stem with Lian Zhen star is Hua Lu (化祿), Jia Heavenly Stem with Po Jun is Hua Quan (化權).

To see things in different perspective, below are the stars and the respective Si Hua.

Star	Hua Lu (化祿) Metal	Hua Quan (化權) Fire	Hua Ke (化科) Wood	Hua Ji (化忌) Water
Northern Star				
Zi Wei	X	Ren	Yi	X
Wu Qu	Ji	Geng	Jia	Ren
Lian Zhen	Jia	X	X	Bing
Tan Lang	Wu	Ji	X	Gui
Ju Men	Xin	Gui	X	Ding
Po Jun	Gui	Jia	X	X
Southern Star				
Tian Ji	Yi	Bing	Ding	Wu
Tian Tong	Bing	Ding	X	Geng
Tian Liang	Ren	Yi	Ji	X
Tian Fu	X	X	X	X
Tian Xiang	X	X	X	X
Qi Sha	X	X	X	X
Centre Star				
Tai Yang	Geng	Xin	X	Jia
Tai Yin	Ding	Wu	Geng, Gui	Yi
Auxiliary Star				
Zuo Fu	X	X	Ren	X
You Bi	X	X	Wu	X
Wen Chang	X	X	Bing	Xin
Wen Qu	X	X	Xin	Ji

Type of Si Hua

There are 3 types of Si Hua based on the Si Hua table mapping above. They are:

- Birth Year Si Hua – this Si Hua is based on the chart of the birth year of the person.

- Self Si Hua – this is when the heavenly stem is the same palace as the Si Hua Zi Wei Dou Shu star.
- Inter-palaces Si Hua – this is when the heavenly stem and Si Hua star are on different palaces.

Example chart as follow:

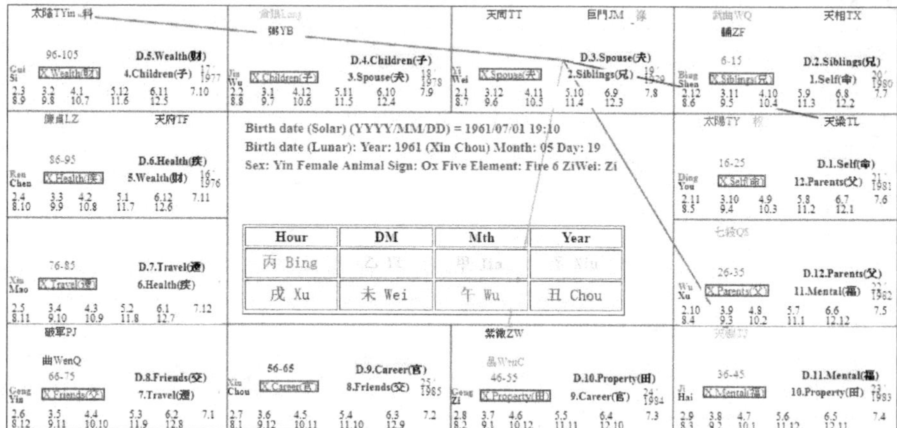

Self Si Hua

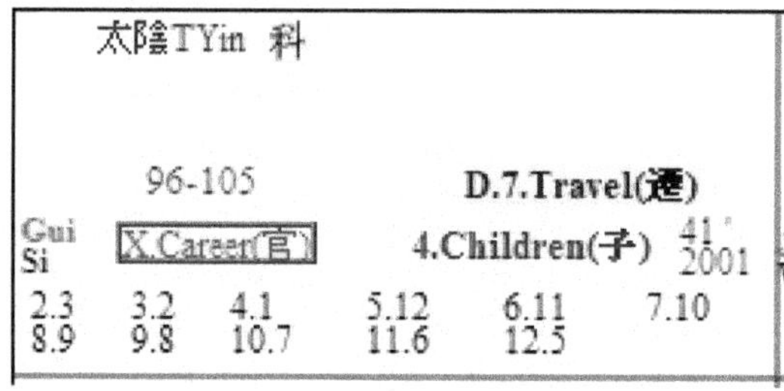

- Gui with Tai Yin is Hua Ke and since it is on same palace, Tai Yin is Self Si Hua.

Birth Year Si Hua

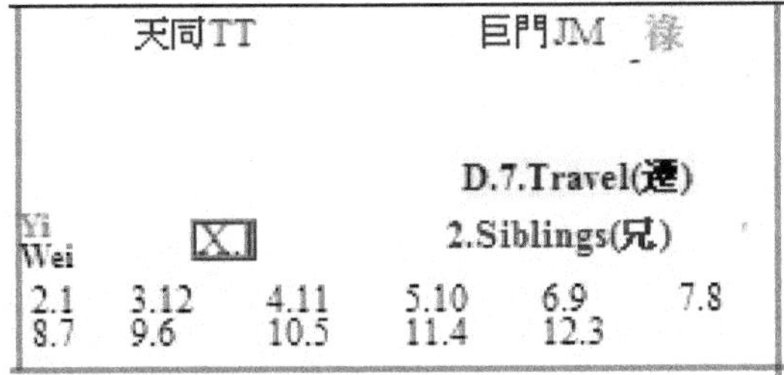

- Birth Year is Xin. Xin Hua Lu at Ju Men star.

Inter Palaces Si Hua

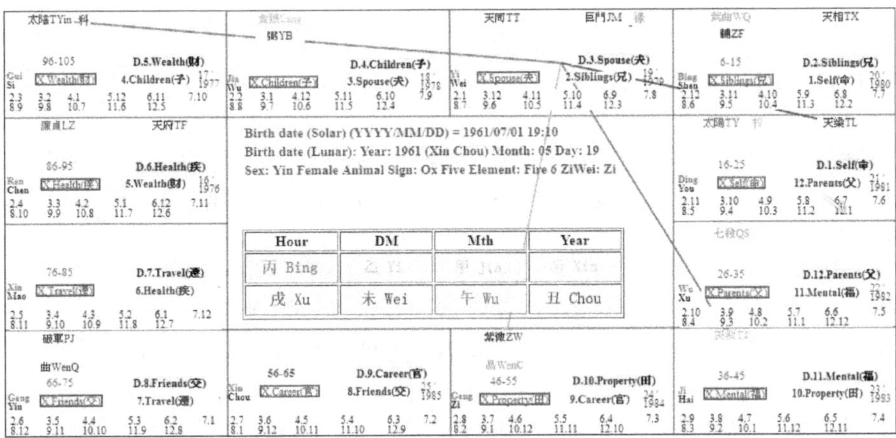

At Siblings Palace:

- Yi Hua Lu to Tian Ji at Property Palace
- Yi Hua Quan to Tian Liang at Parents Palace
- Yi Hua Ke to Zi Wei at Career Palace
- Yi Hua Ji to Tai Yin at Children Palace.

Star Si Hua at Palace:

Self:

Zi Wei (紫微)

Hua Quan: Person is able, strong and in control. If it is with Zuo Fu or You Bi, it will be even more powerful.

Hua Ke: Noblemen will come to help. With the noblemen helping, Zi Wei can then manifest its capability.

Wu Qu (武曲)

Hua Lu: Represents direct wealth, strong character and making money. It is very good for the person to be an entrepreneur or a businessman.

Hua Quan: Represents someone who takes charge. A key person in the company. Good for the person to be in the military service.

Hua Ke: Represents achievements in literature. Good to be involved in literature or art.

Hua Ji: Represent a lot of stress and obstacles.

Lian Zhen (廉贞)

Hua Lu: Represents leadership qualities, and things will be smooth for the person. It also represents peach blossom, so his/her relationships will have many ups and downs.

Hua Ji: Lian Zhen represents feelings, and combined with Hua Ji, it means that the person will want to rebel. Lian Zhen also represents officer star, so when Hua Ji is in Decade or Annual, the person should be careful of legal issues.

Tan Lang (贪狼)

Hua Lu: Represents intelligence, peach blossom and indirect wealth luck.

Hua Quan: Capable, eloquent and will have achievements.

Hua Ji: The person will have a lot of dreams but cannot fulfil them. In addition, people with Tan Lang Hua Ji will get involved in Chinese Meta-Physics.

Ju Men (巨门)

Hua Lu: Eloquent. Together with Wen Chang or Wen Qu, it would mean that the person will have a lot of peach blossom luck.

Hua Quan: Good if the person uses his/her presentation skills to make money.

Hua Ji: Represents gossip and scandal.

Po Jun (破军)

Hua Lu: Changes, wealth luck and good relationships with people in general.

Hua Quan: Represents start-up, which means that the person need to work very hard. The person will succeed if he/ she works hard.

Tian Ji (天机)

Hua Lu: Intelligent, bright and religious.

Hua Quan: Good at strategy, calculative and capable.

Hua Ke: Represents wisdom and intelligence. The person will also be good at painting/drawing.

Hua Ji: The person will not able to see the big picture, and will be sceptical and stubborn.

Tian Tong (天同)

Hua Lu: Good fortune but the person will have a laid back attitude.

Hua Quan: Represents enthusiasm.

Hua Ji: Represents someone that is not good at human to human relationships. The person will also do a sloppy job for his/her tasks.

Tian Liang (天梁)

Hua Lu: Able to overcome calamities.

Hua Quan: Likes to be in control, to meddle with other people's business.

Hua Ke: Likes to do jobs related to research.

Tai Yang (太阳)

Hua Lu: Image of a big boss.

Hua Quan: Firm, sturdy, entrepreneur, stubborn, and will want to win.

Hua Ji: Not good if it is in the male chart as it means that the person will have to work very hard, will easily lose his temper and offend others.

Tai Yin (太阴)

Hua Lu: Represents wealth storage and comfort.

Hua Quan: In a male chart, the man will like to enjoy and be contented with what he has. If it is in a female chart, the woman will be capable and have good communication skills.

Hua Ke: The person will look gentle and delicate and be good at literary arts.

Hua Ji: Not ideal in a female chart, as she will lose more and gain less.

Wen Chang (文昌)

Hua Ke: Talented and intelligent.

Hua Ji: Cocky and overly proud of one's ability.

Wen Qu (文曲)

Hua Ke: Talented in music and art.

Hua Ji: Not good at communication and will easily offend others.

Zuo Fu (左輔)

Hua Ke: Noblemen will come to help the person.

You Bi (右弼)

Hua Ke: Noblemen will secretly help the person.

Siblings:

Zi Wei (紫微)

Hua Quan: Brothers have authority.

Hua Ke: Brothers will take care of the person.

Wu Qu (武曲)

Hua Lu: Brothers have a strong character and are able to make money.

Hua Quan: Siblings like to take charge.

Hua Ke: Will be able to get help from brothers.

Hua Ji: Sibling passed away or siblings will have affinity with religious matters.

Lian Zhen (廉贞)

Hua Lu: Hidden peach blossom, and people from the opposite sex will come and help the person.

Hua Ji: The person will make friends with the wrong type of people and/or get into an affair.

Tan Lang (贪狼)

Hua Lu: Hidden wealth, indirect wealth.

Hua Quan: Siblings are stubborn and overbearing.

Hua Ji: Siblings are emotional and/or proficient in the Chinese five-arts.

Ju Men (巨门)

Hua Lu: Likes to make friends.

Hua Quan: Brothers are eloquent, and if there are arguments, the person will lose out.

Hua Ji: Often have arguments with their siblings or friends.

Po Jun (破军)

Hua Lu: Brothers and friends will take care of you.

Hua Quan: Brothers and friends are the ones in-charge.

Tian Ji (天机)

Hua Lu: Siblings are intelligent and bright.

Hua Quan: Brothers will go through a lot of changes.

Hua Ke: Brothers will be able to teach the person.

Hua Ji: Shallow affinity with their brothers.

Tian Tong (天同)

Hua Lu: Harmonious brothers.

Hua Quan: Siblings are lazy and do not want to take on responsibilities.

Hua Ji: The person will not be on good terms with his/her brothers.

Tian Liang (天梁)

Hua Lu: Brothers and friends will take care of the person, but the person might sometimes feel restricted by them.

Hua Quan: The person will listen to their siblings as their siblings are eloquent.

Hua Ke: Siblings will care for the person.

Tai Yang (太阳)

Hua Lu: If the person partners with others, they will not have the authority.

Hua Quan: Brothers like to show off.

Hua Ji: Brother has passed away or the person will have conflict with his/her brothers or friends.

Tai Yin (太阴)

Hua Lu: Good relationship with sisters.

Hua Quan: Sisters holds the power.

Hua Ke: Good relationship with sisters.

Hua Ji: Sister has passed away or the person will have conflict with his/ her sisters or friends.

Wen Chang (文昌)

Hua Ke: Able to get financial help from siblings and friends.

Hua Ji: The person will have financial conflicts with his/her siblings and friends.

Wen Qu (文曲)

Hua Ke: The person will be able to get financial help from his/her siblings and friends.

Hua Ji: The person will have financial conflicts with his/her siblings and friends.

Zuo Fu (左輔)

Hua Ke: Good affinity with siblings.

You Bi (右弼)

Hua Ke: Good affinity with siblings.

Spouse:

Zi Wei (紫微)

Hua Quan: Good career and family. Spouse holds the power.

Hua Ke: Good career and family. Spouse is considerate and compassionate.

Wu Qu (武曲)

Hua Lu: Spouse has a strong character and is capable.

Hua Quan: Spouse has a strong character. For the male chart, he will be nagged at by his wife.

Hua Ke: Spouse is considerate, compassionate, capable and has a strong character.

Hua Ji: The person will marry late or may not want to get married.

Lian Zhen (廉贞)

Hua Lu: Spouse is good looking/pretty and has good affinity with the opposite sex.

Hua Ji: Relationship is not smooth, and marriage might clash with his/her career, potentially leading to legal issues.

Tan Lang (贪狼)

Hua Lu: Both the spouse and the person will have affinity with the opposite sex.

Hua Quan: During courtship, the spouse will take more initiative.

Hua Ji: Represents peach blossom and the person will have a lot of gossip/scandals. Spouse will like to learn Chinese meta-physics.

Ju Men (巨门)

Hua Lu: Neglect family.

Hua Quan: Spouse is eloquent, and there may be a lot of arguments.

Hua Ji: Spouse and the person will have different opinions. Hua Ji to Spouse will clash career, therefore the person is likely to have scandals/gossip at his/her office.

Po Jun (破军)

Hua Lu: Exciting courtship. Better to get married late.

Hua Quan: Spouse has to work very hard for his/her career.

Tian Ji (天机)

Hua Lu: At work, it will be easy for them to get help from the opposite sex.

Hua Quan: At work, it will be easy for them to get promoted by superiors of the opposite sex.

Hua Ke: At work, it will be easy for them to get favours from the opposite sex.

Hua Ji: Communication problems with the spouse.

Tian Tong (天同)

Hua Lu: Spouse can help them in their career.

Hua Quan: Spouse knows how to enjoy life.

Hua Ji: Relationship with spouse is not harmonious.

Tian Liang (天梁)

Hua Lu: For the male chart, the person will get help from the wife's family. For the female chart, her boss will take care of her.

Hua Quan: Spouse likes to take charge.

Hua Ke: Spouse likes to take charge but will respect the person's opinion.

Tai Yang (太阳)

Hua Lu: For the male chart, the person will be able to get help from his spouse for his career. For the female chart, she has a high chance of becoming the wife of a boss.

Hua Quan: Capable spouse that has power.

Hua Ji: For the female chart, she is not suitable for marriage. For the male chart, as the Spouse palace clashes the Career palace, he is not suitable to start his own business.

Tai Yin (太阴)

Hua Lu: For the male chart, his spouse is capable and compassionate. For the female chart, she will be married into a noble family.

Hua Quan: Capable spouse, good for the person to start his/her own business.

Hua Ke: Gentle and understanding spouse.

Hua Ji: For the male chart, he is not suitable for marriage. For the female chart, she is not suitable to start her own business or she will marry someone who was previously married.

Wen Chang (文昌)

Hua Ke: Spouse is talented in literature and art.

Hua Ji: Spouse will be the type of person that likes to get to the bottom of things.

Wen Qu (文曲)

Hua Ke: Spouse is talented in literature and art.

Hua Ji: Relationship with spouse will have issues related to peach blossom.

Zuo Fu (左輔)

Hua Ke: Spouse emphasises on the mood and feeling in the relationship (e.g. need to be romantic)

You Bi (右弼)

Hua Ke: Spouse emphasises on the mood and feeling in the relationship (e.g. need to be romantic)

Children:

Zi Wei (紫微)

Hua Quan: Children likes to take charge.

Hua Ke: Person will have noble sons.

Wu Qu (武曲)

Hua Lu: Children are intelligent and stubborn and will have the mindset of an entrepreneur.

Hua Quan: Children are firm and honest.

Hua Ke: Children have good financial instincts.

Hua Ji: May have problems when pregnant, and should take extra precautions against miscarriage.

Lian Zhen (廉贞)

Hua Lu: Children are lively and will have affinity with the opposite sex.

Hua Ji: There might be fighting between children or the person might have legal issues related to peach blossom.

Tan Lang (贪狼)

Hua Lu: Children will have good physical condition and strong sexual desire.

Hua Quan: The person might control their children too much, and the children might rebel against them.

Hua Ji: Children is likely to have emotional issues. The person has to be careful of peach blossom.

Ju Men (巨门)

Hua Lu: Children are eloquent.

Hua Quan: Children good at debate.

Hua Ji: The person may have a generation gap with his/her children and may not be able to understand them.

Po Jun (破军)

Hua Lu: Children are extroverted.

Hua Quan: Children are helpful to the family.

Tian Ji (天机)

Hua Lu: Children are lively, agile and intelligent.

Hua Quan: Children are street smart.

Hua Ke: Children are eloquent.

Hua Ji: Children likes to move about, so the parents should take precautions to ensure that they do not get into accidents.

Tian Tong (天同)

Hua Lu: Healthy children.

Hua Quan: Children likes to enjoy.

Hua Ji: The person and his/her children are workaholics.

Tian Liang (天梁)

Hua Lu: Children will have affinity with elders.

Hua Quan: Children are independent and do not want to be controlled by their parents.

Hua Ke: The person will take care of his/her children.

Tai Yang (太阳)

Hua Lu: Children can help the person in his/her career.

Hua Quan: Children can be good helpers.

Hua Ji: Children have to work hard.

Tai Yin (太阴)

Hua Lu: Children are smart and intelligent. The person will be able to accumulate fixed asset.

Hua Quan: Children are hardworking.

Hua Ke: The person will leave some asset for his/her children.

Hua Ji: The person will worry about his/her daughter.

Wen Chang (文昌)

Hua Ke: Children are gentle and demure.

Hua Ji: Children are temperamental or rough.

Wen Qu (文曲)

Hua Ke: Children are gentle and demure.

Hua Ji: The person or his/her children will be vexed because of relationship problems.

Zuo Fu (左輔)

Hua Ke: Children will have good socialising skills. The person will also like people of the opposite sex who are much younger than him/her.

You Bi (右弼)

Hua Ke: Children will have good socialising skills. The person will also like people of the opposite sex who are much younger than him/her.

Wealth:

Zi Wei (紫微)

Hua Quan: Good at money management.

Hua Ke: Will have noblemen coming to help.

Wu Qu (武曲)

Hua Lu: Good at making money.

Hua Quan: Good in finance and will be able to manage wealth well.

Hua Ke: Will have wealth and status.

Hua Ji: Will lose wealth.

Lian Zhen (廉贞)

Hua Lu: Makes money easily, and have stable wealth resources.

Hua Ji: Lose money due to legal issues or due to Peach Blossom.

Tan Lang (贪狼)

Hua Lu: Capable of making money but the person would need to socialise in order to make the money.

Hua Quan: Entrepreneur, good at social communication, and will have a lot of money. For the male chart, he has to be careful of overindulging in sexual pleasures.

Hua Ji: Wealth luck not smooth and the person will lose money because of peach blossom.

Ju Men (巨门)

Hua Lu: Need to be eloquent to make money.

Hua Quan: Should get into a career that requires talking. The person will make money from competition.

Hua Ji: Conflict with others due to money issues.

Po Jun (破军)

Hua Lu: There is accidental wealth.

Hua Quan: Late in obtaining wealth. Need to lose money first before earning more later.

Tian Ji (天机)

Hua Lu: Money comes and goes.

Hua Quan: Good at financial planning.

Hua Ke: Suitable to work in careers related to financial management.

Hua Ji: Suitable to make money from Chinese Meta-Physics.

Tian Tong (天同)

Hua Lu: Lazy to make money.

Hua Quan: Good wealth luck.

Hua Ji: Not easy to make money.

Tian Liang (天梁)

Hua Lu: Need help from elders to earn money.

Hua Quan: If the person works hard, he/she will be rewarded under the guidance of elders.

Hua Ke: When there are problems with money, there will be elders coming to help.

Tai Yang (太阳)

Hua Lu: Can make money but the person needs to live within his/her means.

Hua Quan: For the male chart, it is better to start his own business.

Hua Ji: For the male chart, it is better if he does not start his own business. For the female chart, she lacks affinity with her husband.

Tai Yin (太阴)

Hua Lu: Wealth storage, will get help from the opposite sex.

Hua Quan: For the male chart, he will get help from females to earn money. For the female chart, she can start her own business.

Hua Ke: Suitable to earn money from female-dominated industries. For the male chart, he can get the help of his wife to earn money.

Hua Ji: For the female chart, she is not suitable to start her own business.

Wen Chang (文昌)

Hua Ke: The person will be in situations of having to pay/ be paid in instalments.

Hua Ji: The person's documents, receipts or bills is likely to have problems.

Wen Qu (文曲)

Hua Ke: The person will be in situations of having to pay/ be paid in instalments.

Hua Ji: The person will have relationship problems with people he/she loans money to/ borrows from, and will ultimately lose money.

Zuo Fu (左輔)

Hua Ke: Will have noblemen coming to help when the person has financial issues. The noblemen will help the person openly.

You Bi (右弼)

Hua Ke: Will have noblemen coming to help when the person has financial issues but the nobleman will help the person secretly.

Health:

Zi Wei (紫微)

Hua Quan: Too uptight about illness and in the end, the person would have created an illness out of nothing.

Hua Ke: Will have noblemen coming to help when there is illness.

Wu Qu (武曲)

Hua Lu: Able to control his/her own temper.

Hua Quan: Weak physique.

Hua Ke: Body is able to recover from illness.

Hua Ji: Weak physique, lungs will be especially weak.

Lian Zhen (廉贞)

Hua Lu: The person is sentimental and will have peach blossom(s).

Hua Ji: The person will get into accidents or be involved in peach blossom affairs.

Tan Lang (贪狼)

Hua Lu: The person is sentimental and will have peach blossom(s).

Hua Quan: The person has to be careful of over- indulgence which will be detrimental to the body.

Hua Ji: The person will have a strong sexual desire, and is likely to contract sexually transmitted diseases. The person is also likely to have kidney problems.

Ju Men (巨门)

Hua Lu: The person has gourmet luck.

Hua Quan: The person is not suitable to drink, as he/she is likely to spill out secrets after drinking.

Hua Ji: The person has low alcohol tolerance and is not suitable to drink.

Po Jun (破军)

Hua Lu: The person likes to enjoy, but has to be careful of over spending.

Hua Quan: Emotional because of work.

Tian Ji (天机)

Hua Lu: Intelligent.

Hua Quan: The person is likely to go into research. The person will work overtime for his/her career. He/she needs to take care of his/her liver.

Hua Ke: The person likes to enjoy and relax.

Hua Ji: Likely to have problems with the head.

Tian Tong (天同)

Hua Lu: Body will be fat. Even there is illness, the person will recover fast.

Hua Quan: Body will be large and strong. Around middle- age, the person will start putting on weight.

Hua Ji: Likely to have urinal track problems. For the female chart, she will have an irregular menstruation cycle.

Tian Liang (天梁)

Hua Lu: Will have a healthy and long life. The person will be taken care of by elders.

Hua Quan: Parents will control the person's daily life. The person will feel like he/she does not have any freedom.

Hua Ke: Elders will take care of the person.

Tai Yang (太阳)

Hua Lu: Open minded and will not haggle over small matters.

Hua Quan: Likely to have neck problem.

Hua Ji: The person will have internal conflicts in his/her thinking. Need to be careful of high blood pressure. In addition, he/she needs to take care of his/her eyes.

Tai Yin (太阴)

Hua Lu: Open minded.

Hua Quan: The person will have internal conflicts in his/her thinking due to moral issues.

Hua Ke: For the female chart, she will have someone who will be worried for her health and will take care of her.

Hua Ji: For the male chart, he is likely to have kidney problems. For the female chart, she is likely to have issues related to the female organs. Both the male and female will have issues with their eyes as well.

Wen Chang (文昌)

Hua Ke: Need to listen to doctor's advice.

Hua Ji: Likely to have lung problems and headaches.

Wen Qu (文曲)

Hua Ke: Need to listen to doctor's advice.

Hua Ji: Likely to have heart problems.

Zuo Fu (左輔)

Hua Ke: When sick, will get good doctors.

You Bi (右弼)

Hua Ke: When sick, will get good doctors.

Travel:

Zi Wei (紫微)

Hua Quan: The person will be able to attain great achievements if he/she works overseas. They will receive help from noblemen. They will have status and wealth.

Hua Ke: The person will be able to attain great achievements if he/she works overseas. The person will receive help from noblemen. However, the person will only have status but no wealth.

Wu Qu (武曲)

Hua Lu: Good social communication skills and will be able to settle matters over a meal.

Hua Quan: Able to settle matters just by showing his/her authority.

Hua Ke: Able meet customer during social events.

Hua Ji: Will not get much support when working overseas. He/she will need to rely on him/herself to make money.

Lian Zhen (廉贞)

Hua Lu: The person has strong affinity with people of the opposite sex. When travelling, he/she will get help from people of the opposite sex.

Hua Ji: The person should be careful of legal issues, car accidents, ticket summons or peach blossom disputes.

Tan Lang (贪狼)

Hua Lu: The person has strong affinity with people of the opposite sex. When travelling, he/she will get help from people of the opposite sex.

Hua Quan: The person is active and aggressive and will have good affinity with people of the opposite sex. Thus, the person needs to be careful of getting into illicit relationships.

Hua Ji: When travelling, the person needs to be careful of losing money due to vice activities or disputes related to peach blossom.

Ju Men (巨门)

Hua Lu: The person is good at entertaining but will need to be careful of the friends that he/she meets during entertainment events (e.g partying, networking).

Hua Quan: The person has good communication skills, which he should leverage on for his/her profession. The person will need to pay attention to the language used as he/she might offend others.

Hua Ji: The person should be careful of gossip and scandals.

Po Jun (破军)

Hua Lu: The person has affinity with people, and will make friends with people from all over the world.

Hua Quan: The person will always be travelling.

Tian Ji (天机)

Hua Lu: The person needs to move about and cannot stay in one place long.

Hua Quan: The person will travel a lot.

Hua Ke: The person will have the chance to go for holidays overseas.

Hua Ji: Potential for traffic accidents, external injuries.

Tian Tong (天同)

Hua Lu: When working in a place different from what is normal, (i.e different office, on-site work, different country/state), the person will not be very meticulous.

Hua Quan: The person will have a lot of friends.

Hua Ji: The person will not be able to coordinate properly when working in a place different from what is normal, (i.e different office, on-site work, different country/state). The person should be careful of being a victim of petty crime.

Tian Liang (天梁)

Hua Lu: The person will experience help when overseas but he/she should not take advantage of it.

Hua Quan: When working in a place different from what is normal, (i.e different office, on-site work, different country/state) the person will want to be in-charge.

Hua Ke: The person will have the opportunity to be in-charge.

Tai Yang (太阳)

Hua Lu: Prideful and likes to socialise.

Hua Quan: For the male chart, it is better for him to start his own business. For the female chart, she will have to work in a male-dominated industries to earn money (E.g sports, construction).

Hua Ji: When working in a place different from what is normal, (i.e different office, on-site work, different country/state) the person will need to work hard. If it clashes with the Self Palace, there will be gossip.

Tai Yin (太阴)

Hua Lu: Likes to go on holidays and be close to nature.

Hua Quan: When working in a place different from what is normal, (i.e different office, on-site work, different country/state) the person will have female friends coming to help.

Hua Ke: When going on holidays, there is chance that the person will meet someone he/she already knows.

Hua Ji: When working in a place different from what is normal, (i.e different office, on-site work, different country/state) the person is likely to encounter petty people, especially petty females.

Wen Chang (文昌)

Hua Ke: If the person works overseas, he/she has the chance to migrate there.

Hua Ji: When travelling, the person needs to be careful of being conned or getting involved in disputes.

Wen Qu (文曲)

Hua Ke: If the person works overseas, he/she has the chance to migrate there.

Hua Ji: When traveling, the person needs to be careful of disputes related to relationships or contract.

Zuo Fu (左辅)

Hua Ke: The person will be able to get help from colleagues.

You Bi (右弼)

Hua Ke: The person will be able to get help from colleagues.

Friends:

Zi Wei (紫微)

Hua Quan: Likely to have friends that are in the army or police force.

Hua Ke: Likely to have friends that are in official positions.

Wu Qu (武曲)

Hua Lu: It will be good for the person to talk business over meal.

Hua Quan: Likely to have friends with a finance background.

Hua Ke: Will easily meet new friends during social events.

Hua Ji: The person should be careful of friends that are temperamental. If there is a dispute, the person might be placed in an unfavourable situation.

Lian Zhen (廉贞)

Hua Lu: Likes to socialize, might possibly be good friends with prostitutes.

Hua Ji: Likely to have friends that are a bad influence.

Tan Lang (贪狼)

Hua Lu: Generous and hospitable. The person will value friends over family. However, the person needs to be careful of being sabotaged by his/her friends.

Hua Quan: The person will have peach blossom(s), and a lot of friends that he/she made through partying/ entertainment- related events .

Hua Ji: The person is likely to have peach blossoms disputes with friends (i.e friends fighting over the same girl/boy).

Ju Men (巨门)

Hua Lu: The person has gourmet luck (i.e people will buy good food for them), and likes to socialise.

Hua Quan: Likely to have eloquent friends.

Hua Ji: Likely to argue and offend their friends.

Po Jun (破军)

Hua Lu: Have affinity with others, and are likely to have friends that are able to help in times of need.

Hua Quan: Within friends, there will be someone with power.

Tian Ji (天机)

Hua Lu: Have talented friends.

Hua Quan: Have intelligent and scheming friends.

Hua Ke: Have romantic friends.

Hua Ji: Should be careful of scheming friends.

Tian Tong (天同)

Hua Lu: Have loyal friends.

Hua Quan: The person will have a lot of friends from socializing.

Hua Ji: Likely to lose money to friends from their social circle.

Tian Liang (天梁)

Hua Lu: Will be able to obtain help from friends that are powerful.

Hua Quan: Within your circle of friends, there will be a friend who is more powerful than the person.

Hua Ke: The person will have a friend that is more powerful than him/her.

Tai Yang (太阳)

Hua Lu: Has the image of a boss. If the person works for someone, he/she can be a supervisor.

Hua Quan: Has the image of a boss. For the female chart, she will have someone helping her. This person can be in a political or diplomatic career.

Hua Ji: For the male chart, he is not suitable to start his own business. When working, he may run into problems created by another male colleague.

Tai Yin (太阴)

Hua Lu: The person will have help from people of the opposite sex.

Hua Quan: The person will have help from people of the opposite sex. The person will have opinionated friends.

Hua Ke: The person will have help from people of the opposite sex.

Hua Ji: The person should be careful of his/her female friends.

Wen Chang (文昌)

Hua Ke: The person prefers friends that are talented in literature or the arts.

Hua Ji: The person will have conflict with his/her friends, especially with issues regarding contracts and documents.

Wen Qu (文曲)

Hua Ke: The person prefers friends that are talented in literature or the arts.

Hua Ji: The person will have mood problems which would lead to him/her not being on good terms with his/her friends.

Zuo Fu (左輔)

Hua Ke: Meet friends through financial dealings.

You Bi (右弼)

Hua Ke: Meet friends through financial dealings.

Career:

Zi Wei (紫微)

Hua Quan: The person will have real power. Good for promotion.

Hua Ke: It will be good for the person to work in the government. If he/she wants to start his/her own business, it should be related to the government.

Wu Qu (武曲)

Hua Lu: Smooth cash flow. Suitable to be in the finance industry.

Hua Quan: Suitable to be in wealth management for a company (e.g. CFO). It will be especially good for the person to be in the army or finance industry.

Hua Ke: Good for the person to be in the military or finance industry.

Hua Ji: The person will have problems with his/ her cash flow.

Lian Zhen (廉贞)

Hua Lu: Career will be smooth.

Hua Ji: The person should be careful of legal issues during work. Alternatively, the person could be in a profession related to the law.

Tan Lang (贪狼)

Hua Lu: Good indirect wealth. When working, the person will have help from people of the opposite sex.

Hua Quan: The person will mainly have hidden power. For the female chart, she can be in politics.

Hua Ji: Career depends on peach blossom. It is not suitable for the person to be working for the government, as he/she might have integrity issues. For those working, they should be careful of having an affair with someone in the company.

Ju Men (巨门)

Hua Lu: It is better for the person to be in a profession that requires interpersonal communication skills.

Hua Quan: The person has good interpersonal skills, so it would be good for him/her to go into a profession that requires interpersonal skills. When they speak, it carries weight, thus, the person is suitable to be in a profession such as a judge or a teacher.

Hua Ji: For the duration of the person's career, he/she will have a lot of gossip and scandals.

Po Jun (破军)

Hua Lu: The person will easily achieve success in their career if their career requires competition.

Hua Quan: The person will have a lot of changes in career. The person needs to be given full power then he/she will not over work.

Tian Ji (天机)

Hua Lu: Good to work in the industry that requires intelligence and analysis (e.g. Research and analysis area).

Hua Quan: Good to use wisdom and intelligence to start his/her own business.

Hua Ke: Good to work in the industry that requires a lot of brain power.

Hua Ji: Not suitable to work in the industry that requires a lot of brain power.

Tian Tong (天同)

Hua Lu: Makes money easily but will become complacent and overly dependent on his/her wealth luck.

Hua Quan: Can depend on networking to start his/her own business.

Hua Ji: Failed business because of relationship or cash flow issues.

Tian Liang (天梁)

Hua Lu: Favoured by the boss and will get promoted easily.

Hua Quan: Good at management.

Hua Ke: Have high status but no power.

Tai Yang (太阳)

Hua Lu: Has the potential to be a boss and will be in control. If working for people, he/she can be a supervisor.

Hua Quan: Has the potential to be a boss and can be in politics. For the female chart, she will have men coming to support and help her.

Hua Ji: For the male chart, he is not suitable to start his own business.

Tai Yin (太阴)

Hua Lu: For the career, he/she will get help from his/her spouse or people of the opposite sex.

Hua Quan: For the female chart, she can start her own business. For the male chart, he will get help from women in setting up his business.

Hua Ke: Spouse can keep money.

Hua Ji: Not suitable to manage fixed asset. When working, the person needs to be careful of his/her female supervisor.

Wen Chang (文昌)

Hua Ke: Good to be in the academic field.

Hua Ji: The person should be careful of contract and document issues.

Wen Qu (文曲)

Hua Ke: Good to be in the academic field.

Hua Ji: The person's skills has no demand due to an overly specialised skill set.

Zuo Fu (左輔)

Hua Ke: Able to get help in the job.

You Bi (右弼)

Hua Ke: Able to get help in the job.

Property:

Zi Wei (紫微)

Hua Quan: House will be clean and beautiful.

Hua Ke: House will have expensive decorations.

Wu Qu (武曲)

Hua Lu: Able to manage his/her ancestor's business.

Hua Quan: The person will like to get solid and sturdy furniture.

Hua Ke: The person will like to stay in a calm and quiet environment.

Hua Ji: Family members will fall out because of money issues.

Lian Zhen (廉贞)

Hua Lu: Good wealth luck.

Hua Ji: When buying property, the person should be careful of the terms and conditions as he/she could have legal issues due to property disputes.

Tan Lang (贪狼)

Hua Lu: Likes to buy luxurious property.

Hua Quan: Likes to decorate the house to make it look very beautiful.

Hua Ji: The person will have a lot of issues related to peach blossoms.

Ju Men (巨门)

Hua Lu: House will have a big kitchen.

Hua Quan: The person likes to give their opinions to his/her family members.

Hua Ji: The person should be careful of the relationship between them and his/her family members.

Po Jun (破军)

Hua Lu: The person might impulsively buy a big house, so he/she should pay attention to the budget when buying a house.

Hua Quan: The person will want to renovate his/her own house.

Tian Ji (天机)

Hua Lu: The more the person changes his/her property, the bigger it will get.

Hua Quan: A lot of emphasis on the decorations in the house.

Hua Ke: Spend a lot of money on house decorations.

Hua Ji: The person will be vexed over the renovations and decorations in the house.

Tian Tong (天同)

Hua Lu: The person will have a chance to buy a luxurious home.

Hua Quan: The person likes to buy good quality furniture and appliances.

Hua Ji: The person will often have problems with water and electrical appliances in his/her house.

Tian Liang (天梁)

Hua Lu: Family members will get along very well.

Hua Quan: Likes to be in charge at home.

Hua Ke: Everything will be stable for the person when he/she grows old.

Tai Yang (太阳)

Hua Lu: The person will first form a family before having success in his/her career.

Hua Quan: The person likes people to visit him/her at home.

Hua Ji: Male owner of the property has to work very hard. The house will be a bit dark/gloomy.

Tai Yin (太阴)

Hua Lu: The person will have a lot of fixed asset. He/she is suitable to be in careers related to fixed asset management.

Hua Quan: In the household, the female will take charge.

Hua Ke: The house looks very romantic.

Hua Ji: Female owner of the house has to work very hard.

Wen Chang (文昌)

Hua Ke: The person is likely to buy property through instalments.

Hua Ji: The person should be careful with the documentation and contract of his/her properties. Also, he/she is not suitable to be a guarantor.

Wen Qu (文曲)

Hua Ke: The person is likely to buy property through instalments.

Hua Ji: The person should be careful with the documentation and contract of his/her properties. Also, he/she is not suitable to be a guarantor.

Zuo Fu (左輔)

Hua Ke: Likes to stay in the academic area (e.g near schools).

You Bi (右弼)

Hua Ke: Likes to stay in the academic area (e.g near schools).

Mental:

Zi Wei (紫微)

Hua Quan: When old, he/she will like to enjoy a quiet life.

Hua Ke: When old, he/she will have grandchildren to accompany them.

Wu Qu (武曲)

Hua Lu: When old, he/she would not have to worry about money.

Hua Quan: When old, he/she will be able to control his/her wealth.

Hua Ke: The person will take care of his/her children. When old, he/she will be able to control his/her wealth.

Hua Ji: When old, he/she will worry a lot due to the lack of self-confidence.

Lian Zhen (廉贞)

Hua Lu: When old, he/she would like to enjoy life, and knows how to pamper him/herself.

Hua Ji : When old, he/she will be more emotional and get jealous easily.

Tan Lang (贪狼)

Hua Lu: The person will live a long life with good health.

Hua Quan: When old, he/she will have gourmet luck. This also means that he/she will get into many relationships when he/she is older.

Hua Ji: When old, he/she should be careful of kidney problems. For the female chart, she should be careful of problems with her female organs.

Ju Men (巨门)

Hua Lu: Good gourmet luck.

Hua Quan: When old, the person is unable to let go of his/her past fame and status. The person will also worry too much about everything.

Hua Ji: When old, he/she will not have gourmet luck. The person should be careful of his/her food intake as it might cause health issues.

Po Jun (破军)

Hua Lu: Likes to enjoy, especially with expensive things.

Hua Quan: Likes luxurious and extravagant things.

Tian Ji (天机)

Hua Lu: The person will be able to plan for his/her old age. The person likes religious study.

Hua Quan: The person likes to seek knowledge especially in the Chinese five-arts

Hua Ke: When old, he/she will get involved in religious matters.

Hua Ji: When old, the/she will become more religious.

Tian Tong (天同)

Hua Lu: Likes to enjoy life and he/she will live a long life.

Hua Quan: The person will live a long life and is good at maintaining his/her health.

Hua Ji: When old, will have a lot of illnesses.

Tian Liang (天梁)

Hua Lu: The person will live a long and healthy life.

Hua Quan: Likes to be flattered by juniors. When old, the person will like to study.

Hua Ke: The person will like to take care of people of a lower status than them (juniors), or when he/she is old, he/she will take care of his/her grandchildren.

Tai Yang (太阳)

Hua Lu: When old, he/she will become more optimistic.

Hua Quan: When old, he/she will like to socialise and have a lot of friends.

Hua Ji: When old, he/she will become more emotional.

Tai Yin (太阴)

Hua Lu: Able to accumulate wealth.

Hua Quan: When old, he/she will have better love affinity.

Hua Ke: When old, the/she will have better love affinity.

Hua Ji: When old, he/she will like to live alone, and will not want to communicate with his/her children.

Wen Chang (文昌)

Hua Ke: When old, he/she will be interested in philosophy study.

Hua Ji: When old, he/she will be easily agitated. The person will like to take advantage of his position as a senior to throw his/her weight around.

Wen Qu (文曲)

Hua Ke: When old, he/she will be interested in the study of philosophy.

Hua Ji: When old, he/she will be easily agitated. The person will like to take advantage of his position as a senior to throw his/her weight around.

Zuo Fu (左輔)

Hua Ke: When old, he/she will have a very good social life.

You Bi (右弼)

Hua Ke: When old, he/she will have a very good social life.

Parents:

Zi Wei (紫微)

Hua Quan: Noble parents that will be able to help him/her, but it will affect his/her ability to be independent.

Hua Ke: Will have a good relationship with his/her parents.

Wu Qu (武曲)

Hua Lu: Parents know how to make money.

Hua Quan: Parents control wealth.

Hua Ke: Parents will leave their wealth to the person.

Hua Ji: Parents have bad temper.

Lian Zhen (廉贞)

Hua Lu: Good affinity with elders, especially elders of the opposite sex.

Hua Ji: Emotional parents or when his/ her parents were young they were flirty.

Tan Lang (贪狼)

Hua Lu: Parents will live a long life.

Hua Quan: Parents are frank and open- minded.

Hua Ji: Parents are romantic or unrealistic.

Ju Men (巨门)

Hua Lu: Close relationship with parents.

Hua Quan: Parents are involved in gossip/scandals. The atmosphere in the household will not be good.

Hua Ji: There is a generation gap with parents.

Po Jun (破军)

Hua Lu: Parents are egoistic.

Hua Quan: The person's parents will take care of their parents. Furthermore, the person's parents will also have a very strong character.

Tian Ji (天机)

Hua Lu: Has affinity with male elders.

Hua Quan: Parents are capable.

Hua Ke: Parents are bright and intelligent.

Hua Ji: The person will not be close with his/her parents.

Tian Tong (天同)

Hua Lu: Parents will take care of the person.

Hua Quan: Parents will live a long life.

Hua Ji: Parents will work very hard and not know how to enjoy life, or the parents might have health issues.

Tian Liang (天梁)

Hua Lu: Parents love the person very much.

Hua Quan: Parents will have power and status and the person will admire them.

Hua Ke: Parents will take care of the person.

Tai Yang (太阳)

Hua Lu: When old, life will be smooth.

Hua Quan: When old age, he/she will like to socialise.

Hua Ji: When old, he/she will become emotional and may have a bad temperament.

Tai Yin (太阴)

Hua Lu: The person will be closer to his/her mother.

Hua Quan: The person will have an overbearing mother.

Hua Ke: The person will be very close to his/her mother.

Hua Ji: The person will not be close to his/her mother or he/she will have a strict upbringing.

Wen Chang (文昌)

Hua Ke: The person will have a chance of getting inheritance.

Hua Ji: The person is strong and independent, and will not want to depends on his/her parents.

Wen Qu (文曲)

Hua Ke: The person will have a chance of getting inheritance.

Hua Ji: The person is strong and independent, and will not want to depends on his/her parents.

Zuo Fu (左辅)

Hua Ke: The person's relationship with his/ her parents will be like with friends.

You Bi (右弼)

Hua Ke: The person's relationship with his/her parents will be like with friends.

The Multiple layers of a chart

There are multiple layers in a Zi Wei Dou Shu chart. In a nutshell, the layers are:

Chart	Description
Natal Chart	Static chart derived from your birth date and time
Decade Chart	One Decade = 10 years. The decade chart is dynamic and will change every 10 years.
Yearly Chart	The Yearly chart is based on the year cycle.

In addition, each of the 12 palaces in the chart can be inter-use for different layers of interpretation. For example, the Friends Palace also represents your boss because Friends Palace = Career's Parents.

Siblings	Self	Parents	Mental
Spouse	**Natal Chart**		Property
Children			Career
Wealth	Health	Travel	Friends

Siblings (Health)	Self (Wealth)	Parents (Children)	Mental (Spouse)
Spouse (Travel)	**Natal Chart inter use with Career**		Property (Siblings)
Children (Friends)			Career (Self)
Wealth (Career)	Health (Property)	Travel (Mental)	Friends (Parents)

Natal Chart	Career's
Career	Self
Property	Siblings
Mental	Spouse
Parents	Children
Self	Wealth
Siblings	Health
Spouse	Travel
Children	Friends
Wealth	Career
Health	Property
Travel	Mental
Friends	Parents

This concept is called Palace Interchange or Palace overlap.

Palace Interchange (宮位重叠)

Siblings		
Natal	**Siblings**	**Comment**
Siblings	Self	
Spouse	Siblings	
Children	Spouse	
Wealth	Children	Sibling's Accident Thread
Health	Wealth	
Travel	Health	
Friends	Travel	
Career	Friends	
Property	Career	
Mental	Property	Sibling's Accident Thread
Parents	Mental	
Self	Parents	

Spouse		
Natal	**Spouse**	**Comment**
Spouse	Self	
Children	Siblings	
Wealth	Spouse	Relationship with Spouse
Health	Children	Spouse's Accident Thread
Travel	Wealth	Spouse's Wealth (Hua Lu out, wealth comes from wife, Hua Ji in, wealth goes to wife)
Friends	Health	Spouse's Health
Career	Travel	
Property	Friends	
Mental	Career	
Parents	Property	Spouse's Accident Thread
Self	Mental	
Siblings	Parents	Parents-in-law

Children		
Natal	**Children**	**Comment**
Children	Self	
Wealth	Siblings	
Health	Spouse	
Travel	Children	Children's Accident Thread
Friends	Wealth	
Career	Health	
Property	Travel	Children's movement (e.g. Having kids)
Mental	Friends	
Parents	Career	
Self	Property	Children's Accident Thread
Siblings	Mental	
Spouse	Parents	

Natal	Wealth	Comment
Wealth		
Wealth	Self	
Health	Siblings	Sibling's Wealth
Travel	Spouse	
Friends	Children	Wealth's Accident Thread
Career	Wealth	
Property	Health	Wealth Condition
Mental	Travel	Indirect Wealth
Parents	Friends	
Self	Career	
Siblings	Property	Wealth's Accident Thread or Personal Bank account or pocket money
Spouse	Mental	Wealth's mental – if Hua Ji clash Wealth – overspending
Children	Parents	

Natal	Health	Comment
Health		
Health	Self	
Travel	Siblings	
Friends	Spouse	
Career	Children	Health's Accident Thread Your room or clothes
Property	Wealth	
Mental	Health	
Parents	Travel	
Self	Friends	
Siblings	Career	
Spouse	Property	Health's Accident Thread
Children	Mental	
Wealth	Parents	

Travel		
Natal	**Travel**	**Comment**
Travel	Self	
Friends	Siblings	
Career	Spouse	
Property	Children	Travel's Accident Thread
Mental	Wealth	Money spent on transportation (to buy car) or money received from overseas
Parents	Health	
Self	Travel	
Siblings	Friends	Represents the other party that knocks you
Spouse	Career	Travel Agent or work overseas
Children	Property	Travel's Accident Thread
Wealth	Mental	
Health	Parents	Authority (Summons authority)

Friends		
Natal	**Friends**	**Comment**
Friends	Self	
Career	Siblings	
Property	Spouse	
Mental	Children	
Parents	Wealth	
Self	Health	Infectious disease that a friend passed to you.
Siblings	Travel	Represents the other party that knocks you
Spouse	Friends	Married candidates
Children	Career	Partnership
Wealth	Property	
Health	Mental	
Travel	Parents	

Career		
Natal	**Career**	**Comment**
Career	Self	
Property	Siblings	Your workplace, also represents retrenchment
Mental	Spouse	
Parents	Children	
Self	Wealth	
Siblings	Health	Your workplace
Spouse	Travel	Work overseas, marketing
Children	Friends	
Wealth	Career	
Health	Property	Workplace condition or business place
Travel	Mental	
Friends	Parents	Your boss

Property		
Natal	**Property**	**Comment**
Property	Self	
Mental	Siblings	
Parents	Spouse	
Self	Children	
Siblings	Wealth	Household expenses
Spouse	Health	Condition of the house (Cleanliness)
Children	Travel	Moving house
Wealth	Friends	
Health	Career	
Travel	Property	Room Moving house
Friends	Mental	
Career	Parents	

Mental		
Natal	**Mental**	**Comment**
Mental	Self	
Parents	Siblings	
Self	Spouse	
Siblings	Children	
Spouse	Wealth	Indirect Wealth (e.g. Lottery, gambling) State of mind (Happy or not happy) Spiritual thinking
Children	Health	Internal thinking Peach blossom
Wealth	Travel	
Health	Friends	Mental's Achievement
Travel	Career	
Friends	Property	
Career	Mental	Mental state of Mental.
Property	Parents	

Parents		
Natal	**Parents**	**Comment**
Parents	Self	Father
Self	Siblings	
Siblings	Spouse	Mother
Spouse	Children	
Children	Wealth	Money from/to Parents Inheritance.
Wealth	Health	Health of Parent (father)
Health	Travel	
Travel	Friends	Someone who adopts you
Friends	Career	

Career	Property	
Property	Mental	
Mental	Parents	

Inter Palace Si Hua

Inter Palace Si Hua is where the one palace "flies" to another palace. When one palace flies to another palace based on Si Hua, it talks about the Yin Yang and the relationship between the two palaces.

Hua Lu (化祿)

Hua Lu means abundant or good returns. It is also represents something that you want and things that concerns you the most. For example, in the Natal Chart, Self Palace Hua Lu to Wealth Palace, it means that you are always worried about wealth/money.

Hua Quan (化權)

Hua Quan means power struggle. Therefore, if one palace Hua Quan to another palace, it represents the transfer of power from one palace to another, and there might be a power struggle between the two during the process.

For example, if Self Palace Hua Quan to Friends, there are a lot of misunderstandings between you and your friends. It also means that you will give-in to your friends.

Hua Ke (化科)

Hua Ke represents nobleman. So, when there is Hua Ke from one palace to another, that means there is a related nobleman coming to help you. For example, in the Natal Chart, when the Children Palace Hua Ke to Self, it means that having children will bring luck to you.

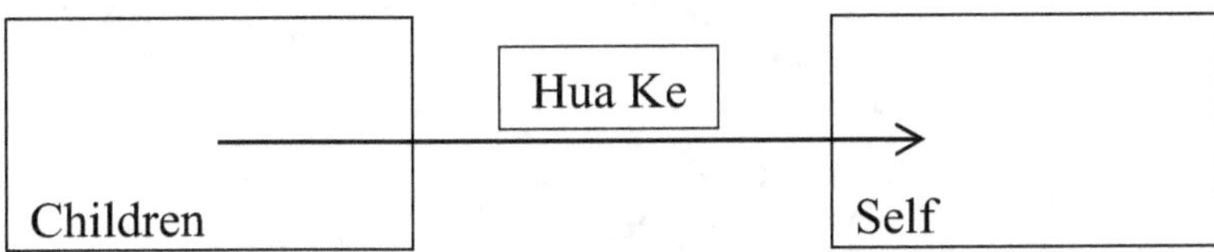

Hua Ji (化忌)

Hua Ji means lacking, fear, dread or abstain. Therefore, if one palace Hua Ji to another palace, it also means it is lacking, or there is no affinity between the two palaces. For example, Self Palace Hua Ji to Parents Palace, it means the person has little or no affinity with his/her Parents.

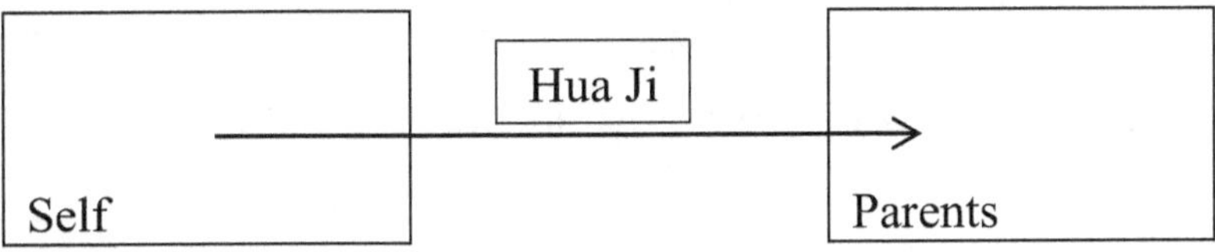

Clash in Si Hua

Clash in Si Hua is normally used in Hua Ji. Clash means it clashes the palace opposite of the palace with Hua Ji. For example:

Yi at Parents Palace Hua Ji at Tai Yin at Children Palace, which will then clash Property Palace (as Property Palace is the opposite of Children Palace). This also means that your parents will not be staying with you.

Ju Men(祿)(權)	Tian Xiang Lian Zhen(祿)	Tian Liang(權)	Qi Sha
2013 / 2025 Gui 14-23 Si Siblings	2014 / 2026 Jia 4-13 Wu Self	2015 / 2027 Yi Wei Parents	2016 / 2028 Bing Shen Mental
Tan Lang Zuo Fu(科) 2012 / 2024 Ren 24-33 Chen Spouse	6th Feb 2011 @16:35, Yin Male, 4th Metal Element		Tian Tong(權) 2017 / 2029 Ding 94-103 You Property
Tai Yin 2011 / 2023 Xin 34-43 Mao Children			Wu Qu You Bi(科) 2018 / 2030 Wu 84-93 Xu Career
Zi Wei Tian Fu Wen Chang(忌) 2022 / 2034 Geng 44-53 Yin Wealth	Tian Ji 2021 / 2033 Xin 54-63 Chou Health	Po Jun Wen Qu(科) 2020 / 2032 Geng 64-73 Zi Travel	Tai Yang(權) 2019 / 2031 Ji 74-83 Hai Friends

In the nutshell, Hua Ji clash refers to rejection and it will have a negative outcome.

Most books will only explain Hua Ji clash. However, it is said that Hua Lu, Hua Quan and Hua Ke can have clash as well.

Inter Chart Si Hua

Inter chart Si Hua is where Decade Chart Si Hua to Natal Chart. This is based on the following phrase in Si Hua Zi Wei Dou Shu:

大限化给本命用，吉凶产生在流年

Meaning: When Decade Chart Si Hua to Natal Chart, auspicious and inauspicious things happens in the Annual Chart.

D.Career	D.Friends	D.Travel	D.Health
D.Property	**Decade Chart**		D.Wealth
D.Mental			D.Children
D.Parents	D.Self	D.Siblings	D.Spouse

Si Hua

Gui Si Siblings	Jia Wu Self	Yi Wei Parents	Bing Shen Mental
Ren Chen Spouse	**Natal Chart**		Ding You Property
Xin Mao Children			Wu Xu Career
Geng Yin Wealth	Xin Chou Health	Geng Zi Travel	Ji Hai Friends

In the nutshell, Decade Chart (Body) Si Hua to Natal Chart (Use). To know when it happens, you have to see the Annual Chart.

For example: Lady Diana chart: Decade 36-45

<table>
<tr><td colspan="2">Gui
Si   D.Travel</td><td>Tan Lang

D.Health</td><td>D.Wealth</td><td>D.Children</td></tr>
<tr><td>D.Friends</td><td colspan="2" rowspan="2" align="center">Decade Chart
36-45</td><td>D.Spouse</td></tr>
<tr><td>D.Career</td><td>D.Siblings</td></tr>
<tr><td>D.Property</td><td>D.Mental</td><td>D.Parents</td><td>D.Self</td></tr>
</table>

<table>
<tr><td>Gui
Si   Children</td><td>Tan Lang
Jia
Wu   Spouse</td><td>Yi
Wei   Siblings</td><td>Bing
Shen   Self</td></tr>
<tr><td>Ren
Chen   Wealth</td><td colspan="2" rowspan="2" align="center">Natal Chart
Lady Diana</td><td>Ding
You   Parents</td></tr>
<tr><td>Xin
Mao   Health</td><td>Wu
Xu   Mental</td></tr>
<tr><td>Geng
Yin   Travel</td><td>Xin
Chou   Friends</td><td>Geng
Zi   Career</td><td>Ji
Hai   Property</td></tr>
</table>

<table>
<tr><td>Gui
Si   A.Career</td><td>Tan Lang
Jia
Wu   A.Friends</td><td>Yi
Wei   A.Travel</td><td>Bing
Shen   A.Health</td></tr>
<tr><td>Ren
Chen   A.Property</td><td colspan="2" rowspan="2" align="center">1997 Annual Chart</td><td>Ding
You   A.Wealth</td></tr>
<tr><td>Xin
Mao   A.Mental</td><td>Wu
Xu   A.Children</td></tr>
<tr><td>Geng
Yin   A.Parents</td><td>Xin
Chou   A. Self</td><td>Geng
Zi   A .Siblings</td><td>Ji
Hai   A.Spouse</td></tr>
</table>

- Gui at Decade Travel Palace Hua Ji to Tan Lang at Spouse Palace, clash Career Palace.
- Overlapping with Annual Chart, it clashes Annual Siblings.
- That year Diana and Dodi were in a car accident in a tunnel along the river Seine in Paris.
- Analysis:
    - It started from Decade Travel, thus, it is related to traffic accident.
    - Using Palace Interchange, Decade Travel Hua Ji clash Natal Spouse-Career thread, which happen to be Health's Children-Property Thread (Health's Accident Thread). This means the Health Palace will have an accident.
    - It also overlap with Annual Friends-siblings Thread, which is Mental's Children-Property Thread. Therefore, she passed away because of an accident.

Part III – Advanced Ingredient

The following sections will provide more information to help in Zi Wei Dou Shu analysis.

Star Structure

Star structure is when a group of stars are in a specific location and configuration. There are more than 60 star structures, and here are the few that are commonly used:

机月同梁 (Jī Yuè Tóng Liáng)

Condition	Tian Ji, Tai Yin, Tian Tong and Tian Liang stars at Self, Career and Wealth Palace.
Result	Good Planner and good in civil service.

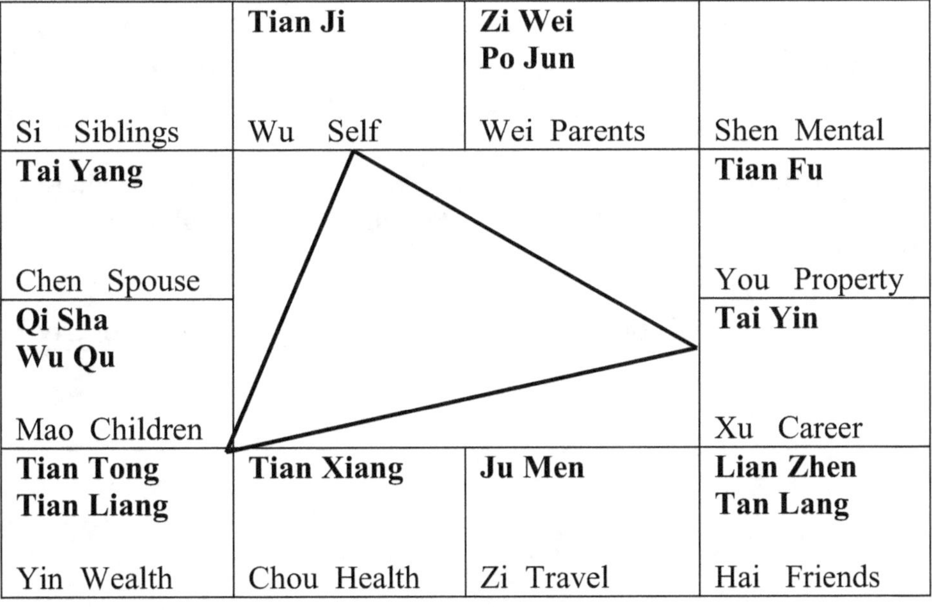

杀破狼 (Shā Pò Láng)

Condition	Qi Sha, Po Jun and Tan Lang standalone at Self, Career and Wealth Palace.
Result	Big changes in life with a lot of ups and downs.

<table>
<tr><td>Ju Men

Si   Children</td><td>Tian Xiang
Lian Zhen

Wu   Spouse</td><td>Tian Liang

Wei   Siblings</td><td>Qi Sha

Shen   Self</td></tr>
<tr><td>Tan Lang

Chen   Wealth</td><td rowspan="2"></td><td rowspan="2"></td><td>Tian Tong

You   Parents</td></tr>
<tr><td>Tai Yin

Mao   Health</td><td>Wu Qu

Xu   Mental</td></tr>
<tr><td>Zi Wei
Tian Fu

Yin   Travel</td><td>Tian Ji

Chou   Friends</td><td>Po Jun

Zi   Career</td><td>Tai Yang

Hai   Property</td></tr>
</table>

府相朝垣（Fǔ Xiāng Cháo Yuan)

Condition	Tian Fu and Tian Xiang without any other stars at Wealth and Career Palace.
Result	All of the basic stuff will be taken care of. Mundane lifestyle.

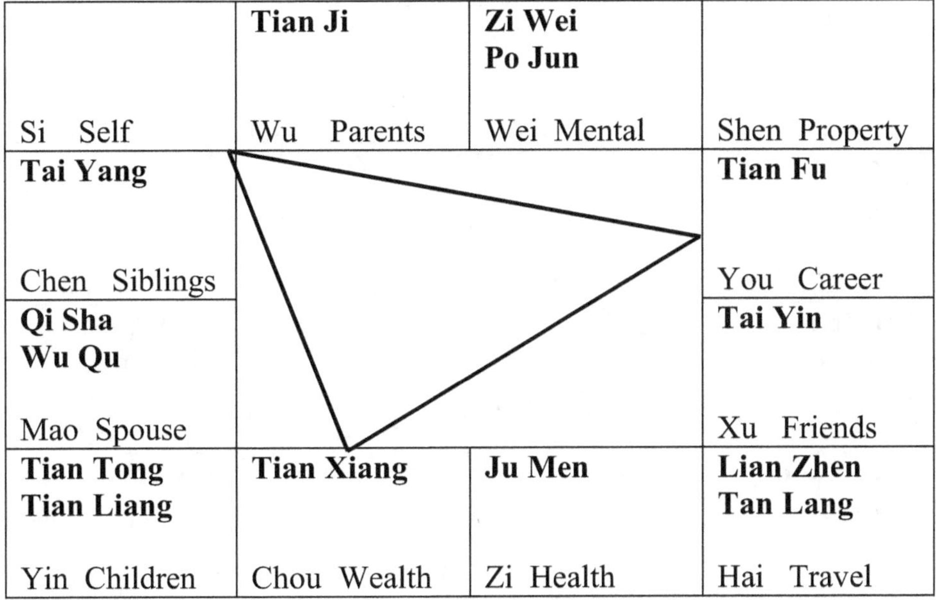

明珠出海 （Míng Zhū Chū Hǎi)

Condition	Tai Yang, Tian Liang and Tai Yin at Career and Wealth Palace. Self Palace must be in Wei Palace.
Result	Early success

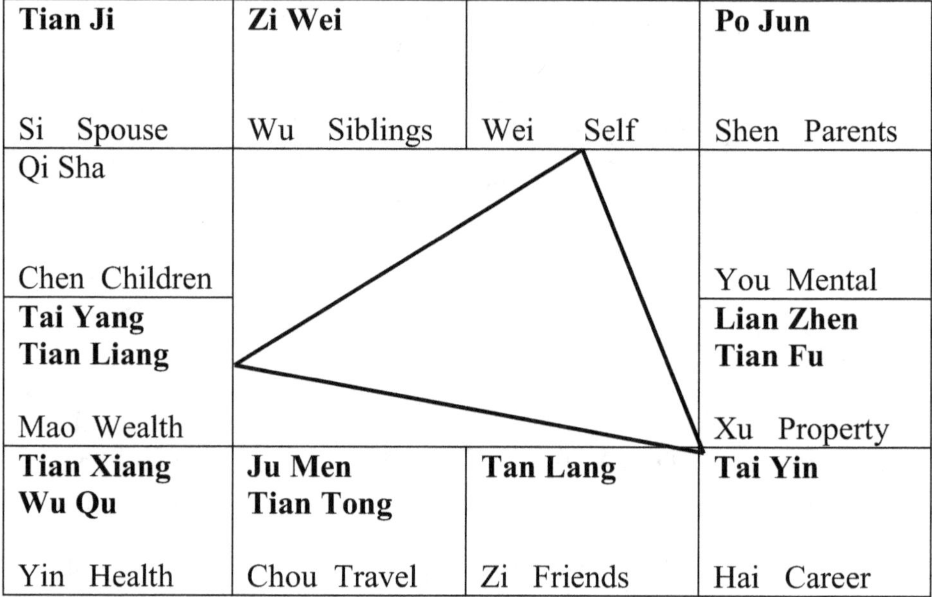

阳梁昌禄 (Yáng Liáng Chāng Lù)

Condition	Tai Yang and/or Tian Liang at Self Palace with Wen Chang and one Hua Lu at Wealth and Career Palace. Self Palace must be in Mao Palace.
Result	Good Academic achievement.

Tian Ji Si Mental	Zi Wei Wu Property	Wen Chang Wei Career	Po Jun Shen Friends
Qi Sha Chen Parents			You Travel
Tai Yang **Tian Liang** Mao Self			**Lian Zhen** **Tian Fu** Xu Health
Tian Xiang **Wu Qu** Yin Siblings	**Ju Men** **Tian Tong** Chou Spouse	**Tan Lang** Zi Children	**Tai Yin (禄)** Hai Wealth

日月照壁 (Rì Yuè Zhào Bì)

Condition	Tai Yin and Tai Yang at Property Palace and Property Palace must at Chou Palace. Both Tai Yin and Tai Yang cannot have Birth Year Hua Ji.
Result	Have many properties.

Tian Liang Si — Health	Qi Sha Wu — Wealth	 Wei — Children	Lian Zhen Shen — Spouse
Zi Wei **Tian Xiang** Chen — Travel	**Zi Wei at Chen**		**You — Siblings**
Ju Men **Tian Ji** Mao — Friends			**Po Jun** Xu — Self
Tan Lang Yin — Career	**Tai Yang** **Tai Yin** Chou — Property	Tian Fu Wu Qu Zi — Mental	Tian Tong Hai — Parents

石中隐玉 （Shí Zhōng Yǐn Yù)

Condition	Ju Men at Zi or Wu Palace.
Result	Start with suffering but will have success in the end. Will have achievements later in life.

<table>
<tr><td>Tai Yin

Si</td><td>Tan Lang

Wu</td><td>Tian Tong
Ju Men

Wei</td><td>Wu Qu
Tian Xiang

Shen</td></tr>
<tr><td>Lian Zhen
Tian Fu

Chen</td><td rowspan="2" colspan="2" align="center">
Zi Wei at Zi
</td><td>Tai Yang
Tian Liang

You</td></tr>
<tr><td>

Mao</td><td>Qi Sha

Xu</td></tr>
<tr><td>Po Jun

Yin</td><td>Chou</td><td>Zi Wei

Zi</td><td>Tian Ji

Hai</td></tr>
</table>

<table>
<tr><td>Si</td><td>Tian Ji

Wu</td><td>Zi Wei
Po Jun

Wei</td><td>Shen</td></tr>
<tr><td>Tai Yang

Chen</td><td rowspan="2" colspan="2" align="center">
Zi Wei at Wei
</td><td>Tian Fu

You</td></tr>
<tr><td>Qi Sha
Wu Qu

Mao</td><td>Tai Yin

Xu</td></tr>
<tr><td>Tian Tong
Tian Liang

Yin</td><td>Tian Xiang

Chou</td><td>Ju Men

Zi</td><td>Lian Zhen
Tan Lang

Hai</td></tr>
</table>

日月反背 （Rì Yuè Fǎn Bèi）

Condition	Tai Yin at Chen Palace and Tai Yang at Xu Palace.
Result	Have a restless lifestyle and is always rushing around.

<table>
<tr><td>Lian Zhen
Tan Lang

Si</td><td>Ju Men

Wu</td><td>Tian Xiang

Wei</td><td>Tian Tong
Tian Liang

Shen</td></tr>
<tr><td>Tai Yin

Chen</td><td colspan="2" rowspan="2">Zi Wei at Chou</td><td>Qi Sha
Wu Qu

You</td></tr>
<tr><td>Tian Fu

Mao</td><td>Tai Yang

Xu</td></tr>
<tr><td>Yin</td><td>Zi Wei
Po Jun

Chou</td><td>Tian Ji

Zi</td><td>Hai</td></tr>
</table>

三奇嘉会 （Sān Qí Jiā Huì)

Condition	Birth Year Hua Lu, Hua Quan and Hua Ke at Self, Wealth and Career palace.
Result	High achievements.

Po Jun **Wu Qu** Si Friends	**Tai Yang** Wu Travel	**Tian Fu** Wei Health	**Tian Ji**(科) **Tai Yin**(祿) Shen Wealth
Tian Tong(權) Chen Career	**Birth Year = Ding**		**Zi Wei** **Tan Lang** You Children
   Mao Property			**Ju Men** Xu Spouse
  Yin Mental	**Lian Zhen** **Qi Sha** Chou Parents	**Tian Liang** Zi Self	**Tian Xiang** Hai Siblings

文桂文华 （Wén Guì Wén Huá)

Condition	Wen Chang and/or Wen Qu inside either Wealth or Career.
Result	Will always have noblemen coming to help.

Wen Qu Si Career	Wu Friends	Wei Travel	Shen Health
Chen Property	**Chou Hour**		**Wen Chang** You Wealth
Mao Mental			Xu Children
Yin Parents	Chou Self	Zi Siblings	Hai Spouse

府弼拱主 （Fǔ Bì Gǒng Zhǔ）

Condition	Zuo Fu and You Bi at either Wealth or Career Palace forming a triangular with Self Palace
Result	Will always have noblemen coming to help.

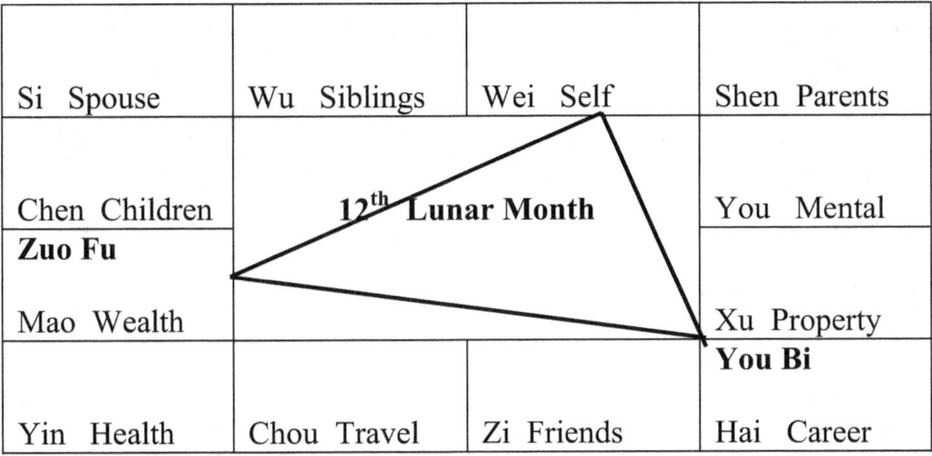

命无正曜 （Mìng Wú Zhèng Yào)

Condition	No major stars inside Self Palace.
Result	Must travel out of birth palace to be successful.

<table>
<tr><td>Po Jun
Wu Qu

Si   Mental</td><td>Tai Yang

Wu   Property</td><td>Tian Fu

Wei   Career</td><td>Tian Ji
Tai Yin

Shen   Friends</td></tr>
<tr><td>Tian Tong

Chen   Parents</td><td rowspan="2"></td><td rowspan="2"></td><td>Zi Wei
Tan Lang

You   Travel</td></tr>
<tr><td>Mao   Self</td><td>Ju Men

Xu   Health</td></tr>
<tr><td>Yin   Siblings</td><td>Lian Zhen
Qi Sha

Chou   Spouse</td><td>Tian Liang

Zi   Children</td><td>Tian Xiang

Hai   Wealth</td></tr>
</table>

Hua Ji Structure

The following are the most common Hua Ji Structure:

射出忌 or 流出忌 (She Chu Ji or Liu Chu Ji)

This happens when Hua Ji originates from the opposite palace as follow:

Palace	Opposite Palace
Zi	Wu
Chou	Wei
Yin	Shen
Mao	You
Chen	Xu
Si	Hai
Wu	Zi
Wei	Chou
Shen	Yin
You	Mao
Xu	Chen
Hai	Si

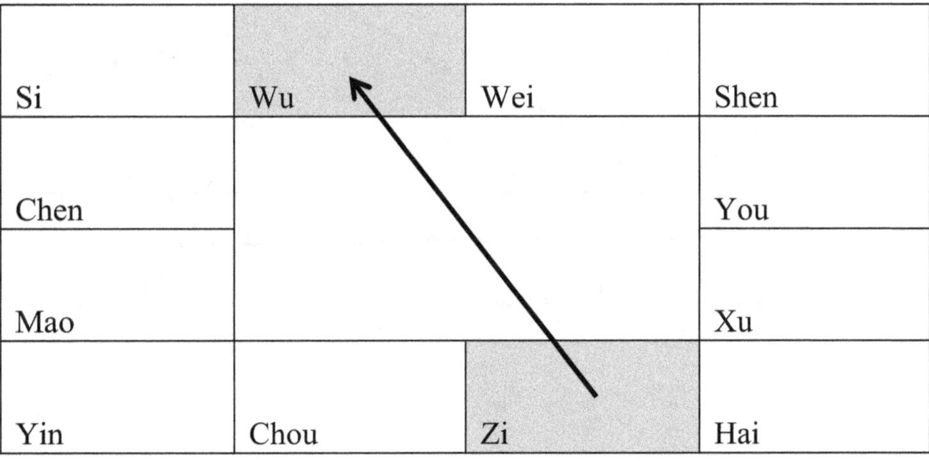

Zi Palace Hua Ji to Wu Palace.

For example, Spouse Hua Ji to Career, Spouse will not like to stay at home. If Wealth Hua Ji to Mental, then the person cannot keep wealth, and will spend money on enjoyment and interests.

水命忌 (Shui Ming Ji)

This is same as She Chu Ji or Liu Chu Ji except that the Self, Wealth, Career or Property Palace Hua Ji to the opposite Palace.

If a person has a chart like this, the person is suitable to work for other people and he/she is should not invest or enter a joint venture with others.

互冲忌 or 纠缠忌 (Hu Chong Ji or Jiu Chan Ji)

This is where both resulting palace clashes with each other. For example, Self Palace Hua Ji to Mental clash Wealth, Friends Hua Ji to Wealth clash Mental. It means that the person is likely to get into misunderstandings with his/her friends due to wealth issues.

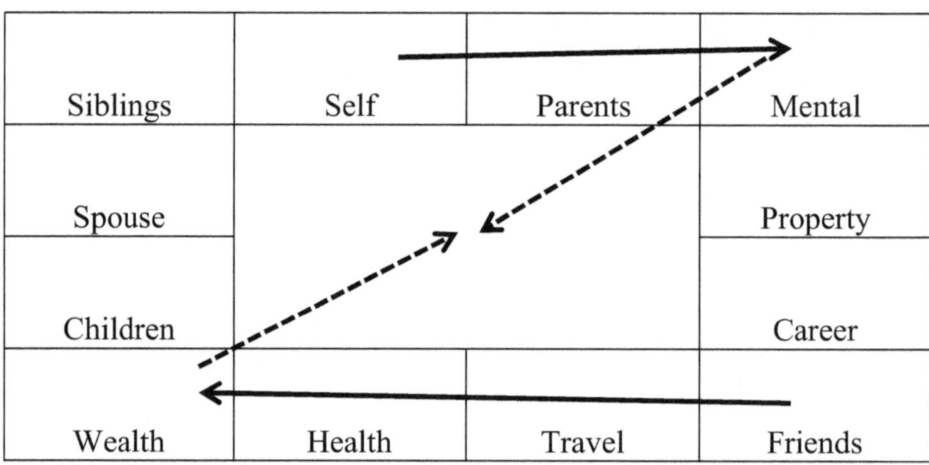

禄来忌 or 是非忌 (Lu Lai Ji or Shi Fei Ji)

No matter what palaces are involved, there will be a disagreement between the palaces. For example, Self Hua Lu to Spouse, Spouse Hua Ji to Self. This will means that "I will treat my spouse well but my spouse will not treat me well".

Siblings *Hua Lu*	Self	Parents	Mental
Spouse *Hua Ji*			Property
Children			Career
Wealth	Health	Travel	Friends

忌来忌 or 循环忌 (Ji Lai Ji or Xun Huan Ji)

This is also known as "an eye for an eye". This means, "how you treat me is how I will treat you". For example, Self Hua Ji to Spouse and Spouse Hua Ji to Self means "If you are good to me, then I will be good to you. If you treat me badly, then I will treat you badly too".

Siblings *Hua Ji*	Self	Parents	Mental
Spouse *Hua Ji*			Property
Children			Career
Wealth	Health	Travel	Friends

反弓忌 or 回力忌 (Fan Gong Ji, Hui Li Ji)

Decade Self, Wealth, Career or Property Hua Ji clash with Natal Self, Wealth Career or Property as Fan Gong Ji.

D.Parents Siblings	D. Mental Self	D.Property Parents	D.Career Mental
D.Self Spouse			D.Friends Property
D.Siblings Children			D.Travel Career
D.Spouse Wealth	D.Children Health	D.Wealth Travel	D.Health Friends

Example: Decade Wealth clash Natal Wealth.

Clash Self or Property: Accident, disaster, lose wealth.
Clash Wealth or Career: Lose wealth, lose career/business.

折马忌 or 四马忌 (Zhe Ma Ji or Si Ma Ji)

Birth Year Hua Ji at 4 horse position, if at Self, it means the person will have a restless life. If at any of the 6-relationship palace (Parent, Spouse, Children Palace), the person will have less affinity with them.

Si	Wu	Wei	Shen
Chen			You
Mao			Xu
Yin	Chou	Zi	Hai

四库忌 or 入库忌 (Si Ku Ji or Ru Ku Ji)

Birth Year Hua Ji at 4 Storage.

Si	Wu	Wei	Shen
Chen			You
Mao			Xu
Yin	Chou	Zi	Hai

Si Ku Ji at Self, Travel, Health, means that the person needs to work hard, rush around, and sacrifice a lot to make a living.

进马忌 (Jin Ma Ji)

Chou Palace Hua Ji to Mao, Mao Palace Self Hua Ji.

Depending on the star, this Ji mainly refers to calamity.

退马忌 (Tui Ma Ji)

Same as Jin Ma Ji, but this is Mao Palace Hua Ji to Chou Palace, Chou Palace Self Hua Ji.

Depending on the star, this Ji mainly refers to calamity.

绝命忌 or 劫数忌 (Jue Ming Ji or Jie Shou Ji)

The palace involved is Self, Wealth, Career, Property. This happens when there is already a Birth Year Hua Ji at any of the previously mentioned palaces and then there is Hua Ji coming into the same palace.

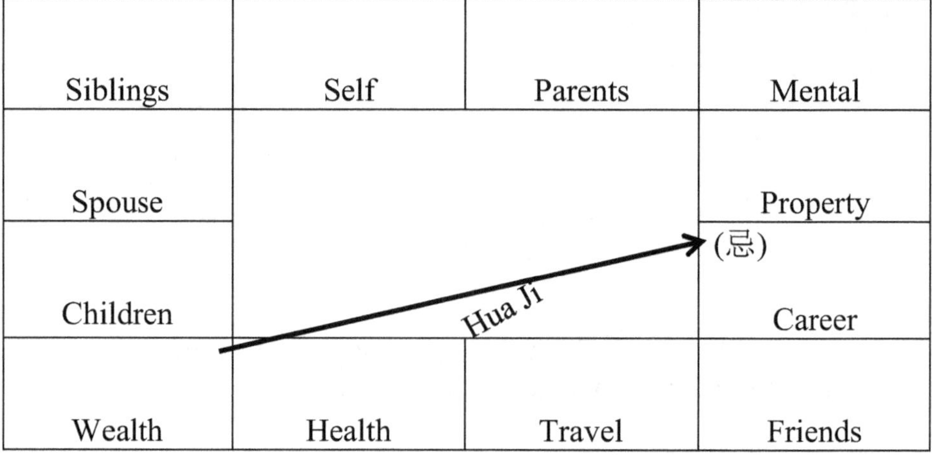

This causes a double whammy to the palace concerned. The result depends on the palace concerned. Need to be careful when the Decade and Annual chart overlaps.

逆水忌 or 回水忌 (Ni Shui Ji or Hui Shui Ji)

This happens when there is a Birth Year Hua Ji at Travel, Mental, or Spouse. On top of that, there is Hua Ji to Travel, Mental or Spouse, which results in a clash to the Self, Wealth and Career Palace.

Siblings	Self	Parents	Mental
Spouse			Property
Children	*Hua Ji*		Career
Wealth	Health	(忌) Travel	Friends

Example: Birth Year Hua Ji at Travel, plus Hua Ji coming in to Travel Palace and clashes Self Palace.

Depending on the star, this Ji mainly refers to calamity.

6-Threads Method (六线法)

The 6-Threads method is the dividing of the 12 Palaces into Yin and Yang. 12 / 2 = 6. Hence, 6-threads method is the Yin Yang derivation of the Zi Wei Dou Shu chart.

Parents – Health thread

Siblings	Self	Parents	Mental
Spouse			Property
Children			Career
Wealth	Health	Travel	Friends

The Parents-Health thread is also known as the Brightness Thread. Using the Natal Chart as an example, the Parents-Health thread shows the quality of the Parent Palace and the Health Palace.

The brightness thread has the following meaning:

- Good luck
- Good prospect
- Upgrade

Using the Palace Interchange concept, using Wealth Palace as the reference point, Wealth Palace Brightness Thread is the Natal chart Children-Property Palace. Therefore, people with good Children and property palace would naturally have good luck or good prospects for their wealth. The same concept can be used for each and every palace in the natal chart.

Self – Travel thread

Siblings	Self	Parents	Mental
Spouse			Property
Children			Career
Wealth	Health	Travel	Friends

The Self – Travel thread is also known as the mobility thread. Using the Natal chart as an example, the Self-Travel thread shows the quality of Self and Travel Palaces.

The mobility thread represents movement and things that are far away. The mobility thread can be applied to Palace Interchange.

Sibling – Friend thread

Siblings	Self	Parents	Mental
Spouse			Property
Children			Career
Wealth	Health	Travel	Friends

The Siblings-Friends thread is also known as the achievement thread. Using the Natal chart as an example, the Sibling-Friends thread shows the quality of the Siblings and Friends Palaces.

The achievement thread has the following meaning:

- Achievement in life
- Good wealth

That means, people with good Siblings and Friends palaces will have good achievement and good wealth.

The achievement thread can be applied to Palace Interchange.

Spouse – Career thread

Siblings	Self	Parents	Mental
Spouse			Property
Children			Career
Wealth	Health	Travel	Friends

The Spouse-Career thread is also known as the emotional thread. Using the Natal chart as an example, the Spouse-Career thread shows the quality of the Spouse Palace and the Career Palace.

The Spouse-Career thread represents the emotional condition of the person.

The emotional thread can be applied to Palace Interchange.

Children – Property thread

Siblings	Self	Parents	Mental
Spouse			Property
Children			Career
Wealth	Health	Travel	Friends

The Children-Property thread is also known as the Peach blossom thread or Accident thread. Using the Natal chart as example, the Children-Property thread is the quality of the Children and Property Palaces.

The Children-Property thread has the following meaning:

- Peach blossom
- Accident

This thread can be applied to Palace Interchange.

Wealth – Mental Thread

Siblings	Self	Parents	Mental
Spouse			Property
Children			Career
Wealth	Health	Travel	Friends

The Wealth-Mental thread is also known as the enjoyment thread. Using the Natal Chart as an example, the Wealth-Mental thread is the quality of the Wealth and Mental Palaces.

The wealth-mental thread has the meaning of enjoyment and appreciation of life.

Stars Combo

Stars combo is when 2 stars appear on the same palace or within the triangle.

The stars combo and meaning is as follow:

Zi Wei + Qi Sha:
The palace where Zi Wei and Qi Sha are together represents the character of the person represented in the palace. For example, if the Self Palace has Zi Wei and Qi Sha, it means that the person has leadership qualities, is benevolent and likes to show off. If Zi Wei and Qi Sha is at the Spouse Palace, then it means that the person's Spouse has the quality.

Zi Wei + Tian Xiang:
Opinionated but often ignored by others as people tend to ignore people with strong opinions.

Zi Wei + Tan Lang:
Represents socializing, lust and desire.

Zi Wei + Tian Fu:
Zi Wei represents starting and Tian Fu represents maintaining. It is better for the person to take up a normal salary job as he/she is not suitable to start or manage a business.

Zi Wei + Po Jun:
It represents enterprising and leadership. The person has to work hard to be successful.

Tian Ji at Mao or You:
A refined person that likes to study Chinese Metaphysics and use their brain power.

Tian Ji + Tai Yin:

If it is in a female chart, she is likely to be involved with a married man.

Tian Ji + Ju Men at Mao or You:

The person should get a job related to the military.

Tian Ji + Tian Liang at Chen or Xu:

The person has affinity with religious matters.

Tian Ji + Ju Men:

In a female chart and if the female is born in Jia or Ding year, her romantic relationships will be complicated and it might be an "unusual relationship" (i.e her husband is of the same age, younger or 7 years older than her).

Tian Ji + Tian Liang:

The person is benevolent, loves to do philanthropy, and has wealth and honour.

Tai Yang + Tian Liang:

If this combination plus Wen Chang or Wen Qu, the person will be successful in national examinations. But this person will have status but no wealth.

Tai Yang + Ju Men:

The person is charismatic, steady, eloquent and able to articulate him/herself well.

Tai Yang + Tai Yin:

The person will be emotional and cold to others. If it is on the Career Palace, the person will sometimes be passive and sometimes active. If it is on the wealth palace, the person is sometimes generous and sometimes stingy. (Emotionally unstable)

Wu Qu + Po Jun:

It is better for the person to be in a specialised field. The person is not suitable to manage a big business and needs to have a specialised skill, especially when the combo is in the Self or Career Palace.

Wu Qu + Qi Sha:

The person is lonely and isolated. The person has strategy but no vision and will do thing boldly and impulsively.

Wu Qu + Tan Lang:

The person is straightforward and enjoys having fun/ partying. He/she will easily get in and out of relationships. His/her life will only be good after 40 years old. If he/she gets rich before 40, then he/she will go bankrupt. If the combination is at the Sibling palace, the person will have a big age gap with his/her siblings. If it is at the Friend Palace, he/she will get to know his/her friends through enjoyment activities or make good friends after 40 years old. Good things comes at a later stage.

Wu Qu + Tian Fu:

Wu Qu is a strong character, whereas Tian Fu is a soft character. Wu Qu represents entrepreneurship and managing money, whereas Tian Fu represents maintaining. This means that the person is good at maintaining wealth.

Tian Tong + Tai Yin at Zi Palace:

Male – handsome and a gentleman; Female- graceful and pretty.

Tian Tong + Tai Yin at Wu:

If born in Bing Year as 马头带剑 (Mǎ Tóu Dài Jiàn – horse head carry a sword). The person is mainly isolated and has a high chance of going overseas.

Tian Tong + Ju Men:

Career that requires talking (e.g. School teacher, salesperson)

Tian Tong + Tai Yin:

Better to go overseas to work.

Lian Zhen + Qi Sha:

Likes to roam about.

Wen Chang + Wen Qu + Lian Zhen:

Will be very poor for a certain period of time but not forever.

Lian Zhen + Tan Lang:

Eloquent and has affinity with peach blossom. The person also does not have his/her own thoughts and are likely to go into mundane careers. (E.g Accountants)

Lian Zhen + Tian Fu:

The person is suitable to work in a finance company. His/ her shortcoming is that he/she will be overly cautious, and thus unable to start his/her own business. If this combination is at the Mental palace, it has the image of committing suicide.

Lian Zhen + Qi Sha:

The person will not die at home or/and the person will get into a lawsuit due to document errors.

Lian Zhen + Tian Xiang:

The person will follow everything according to the law (inflexible). The person might easily have lawsuits.

Part IV – The Cooking

The method to plot chart is presented here.

Plot chart

The following are the steps to plotting a chart:
1. Determine the birth year based on 60 JiaZi
2. Determine the Yin Yang
3. Determine the Yin (Tiger) Palace Heavenly Stem
4. Determine the Self Palace and the rest of the 11 palaces
5. Determine the 5-Element
6. Determine the location of the Zi Wei Star
7. Determine the location of other 13 major stars
8. Determine the location of the Zuo Fu and You Bi stars
9. Determine the location of the Wen Chang and Wen Qu stars
10. Determine the birth year Heavenly Stem Si Hua
11. Determine the Decade Cycle
12. Determine the Yearly Cycle
13. Determine the Birth Year Si Hua
14. Determine the Self Si Hua

1. Determine the birth year based on 60 JiaZi

Zi Wei Dou Shu is based on the Chinese Lunisolar Calendar. So, a new year is determined by the first day of the first month of the Chinese Lunisolar Calendar. For example, in 2018, Li Chun starts on 4th Feb at 05:28. 2018 is Wu Xu Year. Therefore, according to Chinese Solar Calendar, Wu Xu Year starts on 4th Feb 2018 at 05:28. However, Chinese New Year starts on 16th Feb 2018. So, according to Zi Wei Dou Shu, Wu Xu Year only starts on 16th Feb 2018.

Here is a table for the 60 Jia Zi for your reference:

Year (Y-M-D)	60 Jia Zi	Year (Y-M-D)	60 Jia Zi
1930-01-30	Geng Wu	1938-01-31	Wu Yin
1931-02-17	Xin Wei	1939-02-19	Ji Mao
1932-02-06	Ren Shen	1940-02-08	Geng Chen
1933-01-26	Gui You	1941-01-27	Xin Si
1934-02-14	Jia Xu	1942-02-15	Ren Wu
1935-02-04	Yi Hai	1943-02-05	Gui Wei

1936-01-24	Bing Zi	1944-01-25	Jia Shen
1937-02-11	Ding Chou	1945-02-13	Yi You

Year (Y-M-D)	60 Jia Zi	Year (Y-M-D)	60 Jia Zi
1946-02-02	Bing Xu	1978-02-07	Wu Wu
1947-01-22	Ding Hai	1979-01-28	Ji Wei
1948-02-10	Wu Zi	1980-02-16	Geng Shen
1949-01-29	Ji Chou	1981-02-05	Xin You
1950-02-17	Geng Yin	1982-01-25	Ren Xu
1951-02-06	Xin Mao	1983-02-13	Gui Hai
1952-01-27	Ren Chen	1984-02-02	Jia Zi
1953-02-14	Gui Si	1985-02-20	Yi Chou
1954-02-03	Jia Wu	1986-02-09	Bing Yin
1955-01-24	Yi Wei	1987-01-29	Ding Mao
1956-02-12	Bing Shen	1988-02-17	Wu Chen
1957-01-31	Ding You	1989-02-06	Ji Si
1958-02-18	Wu Xu	1990-01-27	Geng Wu
1959-02-08	Ji Hai	1991-02-15	Xin Wei
1960-01-28	Geng Zi	1992-02-04	Ren Shen
1961-02-15	Xin Chou	1993-01-23	Gui You
1962-02-05	Ren Yin	1994-02-10	Jia Xu
1963-01-25	Gui Mao	1995-01-31	Yi Hai
1964-02-13	Jia Chen	1996-02-19	Bing Zi
1965-02-02	Yi Si	1997-02-07	Ding Chou
1966-01-21	Bing Wu	1998-01-28	Wu Yin
1967-02-09	Ding Wei	1999-02-16	Ji Mao
1968-01-30	Wu Shen	2000-02-05	Geng Chen
1969-02-17	Ji You	2001-01-24	Xin Si
1970-02-06	Geng Xu	2002-02-12	Ren Wu
1971-01-27	Xin Hai	2003-02-01	Gui Wei
1972-02-15	Ren Zi	2004-01-22	Jia Shen
1973-02-03	Gui Chou	2005-02-09	Yi You
1974-01-23	Jia Yin	2006-01-29	Bing Xu
1975-02-11	Yi Mao	2007-02-18	Ding Hai

1976-01-31	Bing Chen	2008-02-07	Wu Zi
1977-02-18	Ding Si	2009-01-26	Ji Chou

Year (Y-M-D)	60 Jia Zi	Year (Y-M-D)	60 Jia Zi
2010-02-14	Geng Yin	2020-01-25	Geng Zi
2011-02-03	Xin Mao	2021-02-12	Xin Chou
2012-01-23	Ren Chen	2022-02-01	Ren Yin
2013-02-10	Gui Si	2023-01-22	Gui Mao
2014-01-31	Jia Wu	2024-02-10	Jia Chen
2015-02-19	Yi Wei	2025-01-29	Yi Si
2016-02-08	Bing Shen	2026-02-17	Bing Wu
2017-01-28	Ding You	2027-02-06	Ding Wei
2018-02-16	Wu Xu	2028-01-26	Wu Shen
2019-02-05	Ji Hai	2029-02-13	Ji You

For example, if you are born on 1st Feb 2011, then your birth year is **Geng Yin**. If you are born on 3rd Feb 2011, then your birth year is **Xin Mao.** Note that the birth year is consists of Heavenly Stem and Earthly Branch. For example, in **Geng Yin**, **Geng** is the Heavenly Stem and **Yin** is the Earthly Branch.

2. Determine the Yin Yang

Gender	Birth Year Heavenly Stem	Yin Yang
Male	Jia, Bing, Wu, Geng or Ren	Yang Male
Male	Yi, Ding, Ji, Xin or Gui	Yin Male
Female	Jia, Bing, Wu, Geng or Ren	Yang Female
Female	Yi, Ding, Ji, Xin or Gui	Yin Female

For example, for a male born on 6th Feb 2011, Xin Mao Year, the Yin Yang is Yin Male.

3. Determine the Yin (Tiger) Palace Heavenly Stem

Birth Year Heavenly Stem	Heavenly Stem for Yin (Tiger) Palace
Jia or Ji	Bing
Yi or Geng	Wu
Bing or Xin	Geng
Ding or Ren	Ren
Wu or Gui	Jia

Heavenly Stem runs clockwise from Yin (Tiger) Palace with the following sequence:

Jia -> Yi -> Bing -> Ding -> Wu -> Ji -> Geng -> Xin -> Ren -> Gui

For example, for someone born on 6th Feb 2011, the birth year is **Xin Mao**. Based on the table above, the Heavenly Stem for Yin (Tiger) palace is **Geng.**

Gui Si	Jia Wu	Yi Wei	Bing Shen
Ren Chen			Ding You
Xin Mao			Wu Xu
Geng Yin	Yi Chou	Jia Zi	Ji Hai

4. Determine the Self Palace and the rest of the 11 palaces

The Self Palace is based on two components:

- Lunar Birth Month
- Birth Hour

A. Determine the Lunar Birth Month

There are many tools on the internet that you can use to convert your birth date to the lunar birth date. You can go to my website: http://www.fengshui-hacks.com/, click on Plot Chart, and select ZiWei for Chart.

Birth date (Solar) (YYYY/MM/DD) = 2011/02/06 16:35
Birth date (Lunar): Year: 2011 (Xin Mao) Month: 01 Day: 4
Sex: Yin Male Animal Sign: Rabbit Five Element: Metal 4 ZiWei: Yin

Alternatively, you can refer to the Appendix for the list of the 1st day of a Lunar month.

For example:

2011-01-04	2010-12-01	No
2011-02-03	2011-01-01	No
2011-03-05	2011-02-01	No

- 4th Jan 2011 = 1st Day of 12th Lunar Month, 2010
- 3rd Feb 2011 = 1st Day of 1st Lunar Month, 2011
- 5th Mar 2011 = 1st Day of 2nd Lunar Month, 2011

So, for example, on 6th Feb 2011, the lunar birth month is 1 and the lunar birth day is 4.

B. Birth Hour

The Birth Hour is based on the following chart:

Time	Earthly Branches	Sequence
23:00 – 00:59	子(Zi)	1
01:00 – 02:59	丑(Chou)	2

03:00 – 04:59	寅(Yin)	3
05:00 – 06:59	卯(Mao)	4
07:00 – 08:59	辰(Chen)	5
09:00 – 10:59	巳(Si)	6
11:00 – 12:59	午(Wu)	7
13:00 – 14:59	未(Wei)	8
15:00 – 16:59	申(Shen)	9
17:00 – 18:59	酉(You)	10
19:00 – 20:59	戌(Xu)	11
21:00 – 22:59	亥(Hai)	12

Steps:

1. Starting from Yin (Tiger) Palace, count in a clockwise direction, the number of Lunar Month you were born.
2. At the last Palace, count anti-clockwise the number of birth hour sequence.
3. The last palace is the Self Palace.

For example, if someone is born on 6th Feb 2011 at 16:35, the Lunar Month is 1 and Birth Hour Sequence is 9:

Gui Si	Jia Wu	Yi Wei	Bing Shen
Ren Chen	1 Lunar Month		Ding You
Xin Mao			Wu Xu
Geng Yin	Yi Chou	Jia Zi	Ji Hai

Gui Si Self	Jia Wu	Yi Wei	Bing Shen
Ren Chen		9 birth hour sequence	Ding You
Xin Mao			Wu Xu
Geng Yin	Yi Chou	Jia Zi	Ji Hai

The rest of the palaces are arranged in anti-clockwise from Self Palace:

Self ▶Siblings ▶Spouse ▶Children ▶Wealth ▶Health ▶Travel ▶Friends ▶Career ▶Property ▶Mental ▶Parents

Gui Si Siblings	Jia Wu Self	Yi Wei Parents	Bing Shen Mental
Ren Chen Spouse			Ding You Property
Xin Mao Children			Wu Xu Career
Geng Yin Wealth	Yi Chou Health	Jia Zi Travel	Ji Hai Friends

5. Determine the 5-Element

The 5-Element is determined from the Self Palace Heavenly Stem and Earthly Branch with reference to the following table:

EB → HS ↓	Zi/ Chou	Yin/ Mao	Chen/ Si	Wu/ Wei	Shen/ You	Xu/ Hai
Jia Yi	4th	2nd	6th	4th	2nd	6th
Bing Ding	2nd	6th	5th	2nd	6th	5th
Wu Ji	6th	5th	3rd	6th	5th	3rd
Geng Xin	5th	3rd	4th	5th	3rd	4th
Ren Gui	3rd	4th	2nd	3rd	4th	2nd

Reference	Element
2nd	Water
3rd	Wood
4th	Metal
5th	Earth
6th	Fire

From the example above, the Self Palace is Jia Wu, so the 5-Element is **4th Metal.**

6. Determine the location of the Zi Wei Star

The location of Zi Wei Star is determined by 5-Element and Lunar Birth Date with reference to the following chart:

Birth Date	2nd	3rd	4th	5th	6th
1	Chou	Chen	Hai	Wu	You
2	Yin	Chou	Chen	Hai	Wu
3	Yin	Yin	Chou	Chen	Hai
4	Mao	Si	Yin	Chou	Chen
5	Mao	Yin	Zi	Yin	Chou
6	Chen	Mao	Si	Wei	Yin
7	Chen	Wu	Yin	Zi	Xu
8	Si	Mao	Mao	Si	Wei
9	Si	Chen	Chou	Yin	Zi
10	Wu	Wei	Wu	Mao	Si
11	Wu	Chen	Mao	Shen	Yin
12	Wei	Si	Chen	Chou	Mao
13	Wei	Shen	Yin	Wu	Hai
14	Shen	Si	Wei	Mao	Shen
15	Shen	Wu	Chen	Chen	Chou
16	You	You	Si	You	Wu
17	You	Wu	Mao	Yin	Mao
18	Xu	Wei	Shen	Wei	Chen
19	Xu	Xu	Si	Chen	Zi
20	Hai	Wei	Wu	Si	You
21	Hai	Shen	Chen	Chen	Yin
22	Zi	Hai	You	Mao	Wei
23	Zi	Shen	Wu	Shen	Chen
24	Chou	You	Wei	Si	Si
25	Chou	Zi	Si	Wu	Chou
26	Yin	You	Xu	Hai	Xu
27	Yin	Xu	Wei	Chen	Mao
28	Mao	Chou	Shen	You	Shen
29	Mao	Xu	Wu	Wu	Si

| 30 | Chen | Hai | Hai | Wei | Wei |

From the example, on 6th Feb 2011 at 16:35, the 5-Element is 4th Metal, and the Lunar Birth Date is 1. So, the Zi Wei Star is at Yin Palace.

7. Determine the location of other 13 major stars

Once the Zi Wei Star is determined, the rest of the stars can be determined based on the location of the Zi Wei Star.

Zi Wei at Zi

Tai Yin Si	Tan Lang Wu	Tian Tong Ju Men Wei	Wu Qu Tian Xiang Shen
Lian Zhen Tian Fu Chen			Tai Yang Tian Liang You
  Mao	**Zi Wei at Zi**		Qi Sha Xu
Po Jun Yin	Chou	Zi Wei Zi	Tian Ji Hai

Zi Wei at Chou

Lian Zhen Tan Lang Si	Ju Men Wu	Tian Xiang Wei	Tian Tong Tian Liang Shen
Tai Yin Chen	Zi Wei at Chou		Qi Sha Wu Qu You
Tian Fu Mao			Tai Yang Xu
  Yin	Zi Wei Po Jun Chou	Tian Ji Zi	 Hai

Zi Wei at Yin

Ju Men Si	Tian Xiang Lian Zhen Wu	Tian Liang Wei	Qi Sha Shen
Tan Lang Chen	Zi Wei at Yin		Tian Tong You
Tai Yin Mao			Wu Qu Xu
Zi Wei Tian Fu Yin	Tian Ji Chou	Po Jun Zi	Tai Yang Hai

Zi Wei at Mao

Tian Xiang Si	Tian Liang Wu	Qi Sha Lian Zhen Wei	 Shen
Ju Men Chen	Zi Wei at Mao		You
Zi Wei Tan Lang Mao			Tian Tong Xu
Tai Yin Tian Ji Yin	Tian Fu Chou	Tai Yang Zi	Wu Qu Po Jun Hai

Zi Wei at Chen

Tian Liang Si	Qi Sha Wu	 Wei	Lian Zhen Shen
Zi Wei Tian Xiang Chen	Zi Wei at Chen		You
Ju Men Tian Ji Mao			Po Jun Xu
Tan Lang Yin	Tai Yang Tai Yin Chou	Tian Fu Wu Qu Zi	Tian Tong Hai

Zi Wei at Si

Zi Wei **Qi Sha** Si	 Wu	 Wei	 Shen
Tian Liang **Tian Ji** Chen	**Zi Wei at Si**		**Po Jun** **Lian Zhen** You
Tian Xiang Mao			 Xu
Ju Men **Tai Yang** Yin	**Tan Lang** **Wu Qu** Chou	**Tian Tong** **Tai Yin** Zi	**Tian Fu** Hai

Zi Wei at Wu

Tian Ji Si	**Zi Wei** Wu	 Wei	**Po Jun** Shen
Qi Sha Chen	**Zi Wei at Wu**		 You
Tai Yang **Tian Liang** Mao			**Lian Zhen** **Tian Fu** Xu
Tian Xiang **Wu Qu** Yin	**Ju Men** **Tian Tong** Chou	**Tan Lang** Zi	**Tai Yin** Hai

Zi Wei at Wei

	Tian Ji	Zi Wei Po Jun	
Si	Wu	Wei	Shen
Tai Yang Chen	Zi Wei at Wei		Tian Fu You
Qi Sha Wu Qu Mao			Tai Yin Xu
Tian Tong Tian Liang Yin	Tian Xiang Chou	Ju Men Zi	Lian Zhen Tan Lang Hai

Zi Wei at Shen

Tai Yang Si	Po Jun Wu	Tian Ji Wei	Zi Wei Tian Fu Shen
Wu Qu Chen	Zi Wei at Shen		Tai Yin You
Tian Tong Mao			Tan Lang Xu
Qi Sha Yin	Tian Liang Chou	Lian Zhen Tian Xiang Zi	Ju Men Hai

Zi Wei at You

Po Jun Wu Qu Si	Tai Yang Wu	Tian Fu Wei	Tian Ji Tai Yin Shen
Tian Tong Chen	Zi Wei at You		Zi Wei Tan Lang You
  Mao			Ju Men Xu
 Yin	Lian Zhen Qi Sha Chou	Tian Liang Zi	Tian Xiang Hai

Zi Wei at Xu

Tian Tong Si	Tian Fu Wu Qu Wu	Tai Yang Tai Yin Wei	Tan Lang Shen
Po Jun Chen	Zi Wei at Xu		Tian Ji Ju Men You
  Mao			Zi Wei Tian Xiang Xu
Lian Zhen Yin	 Chou	Qi Sha Zi	Tian Liang Hai

Zi Wei at Hai

Tian Fu Si	Tian Tong Tai Yin Wu	Wu Qu Tan Lang Wei	Tai Yang Ju Men Shen
  Chen	**Zi Wei at Hai**		Tian Xiang You
Po Jun **Lian Zhen** Mao			Tian Ji Tian Liang Xu
  Yin	 Chou	 Zi	Zi Wei Qi Sha Hai

8. Determine the location of the Zuo Fu and You Bi stars

The location of the Zuo Fu and You Bi stars are based on the Lunar Birth Month:

  Si	 Wu	 Wei	 Shen
Zuo Fu Chen	**1st Lunar Month**		You
  Mao			**You Bi** Xu
  Yin	 Chou	 Zi	 Hai

Zuo Fu Si	Wu	Wei	Shen
Chen	2nd Lunar Month		**You Bi** You
Mao			Xu
Yin	Chou	Zi	Hai

Si	**Zuo Fu** Wu	Wei	**You Bi** Shen
Chen	3rd Lunar Month		You
Mao			Xu
Yin	Chou	Zi	Hai

<table>
<tr><td>Si</td><td>Wu</td><td>**Zuo Fu**
You Bi

Wei</td><td>Shen</td></tr>
<tr><td>Chen</td><td colspan="2" rowspan="2" align="center">**4th Lunar Month**</td><td>You</td></tr>
<tr><td>Mao</td><td>Xu</td></tr>
<tr><td>Yin</td><td>Chou</td><td>Zi</td><td>Hai</td></tr>
</table>

<table>
<tr><td>Si</td><td>**You Bi**

Wu</td><td>Wei</td><td>**Zuo Fu**

Shen</td></tr>
<tr><td>Chen</td><td colspan="2" rowspan="2" align="center">**5th Lunar Month**</td><td>You</td></tr>
<tr><td>Mao</td><td>Xu</td></tr>
<tr><td>Yin</td><td>Chou</td><td>Zi</td><td>Hai</td></tr>
</table>

You Bi			
Si	Wu	Wei	Shen
Chen			**Zuo Fu** You
Mao	**6th Lunar Month**		Xu
Yin	Chou	Zi	Hai

Si	Wu	Wei	Shen
You Bi Chen			You
Mao	**7th Lunar Month**		**Zuo Fu** Xu
Yin	Chou	Zi	Hai

<table>
<tr><td>Si</td><td>Wu</td><td>Wei</td><td>Shen</td></tr>
<tr><td>Chen
You Bi

Mao</td><td colspan="2" rowspan="2" align="center">**8th Lunar Month**</td><td>You

Xu
Zuo Fu</td></tr>
<tr><td>Yin</td><td>Chou</td><td>Zi</td><td>Hai</td></tr>
</table>

<table>
<tr><td>Si</td><td>Wu</td><td>Wei</td><td>Shen</td></tr>
<tr><td>Chen

Mao
You Bi</td><td colspan="2" rowspan="2" align="center">**9th Lunar Month**</td><td>You

Xu</td></tr>
<tr><td>Yin</td><td>Chou</td><td>**Zuo Fu**
Zi</td><td>Hai</td></tr>
</table>

<table>
<tr><td>Si</td><td>Wu</td><td>Wei</td><td>Shen</td></tr>
<tr><td>Chen</td><td rowspan="2" colspan="2" align="center">10th Lunar Month</td><td>You</td></tr>
<tr><td>Mao</td><td>Xu</td></tr>
<tr><td>Yin</td><td>Zuo Fu
You Bi
Chou</td><td>Zi</td><td>Hai</td></tr>
</table>

<table>
<tr><td>Si</td><td>Wu</td><td>Wei</td><td>Shen</td></tr>
<tr><td>Chen</td><td rowspan="2" colspan="2" align="center">11th Lunar Month</td><td>You</td></tr>
<tr><td>Mao</td><td>Xu</td></tr>
<tr><td>Zuo Fu
Yin</td><td>Chou</td><td>You Bi
Zi</td><td>Hai</td></tr>
</table>

Si	Wu	Wei	Shen
Chen	**12th Lunar Month**		You
Zuo Fu Mao			Xu
Yin	Chou	Zi	**You Bi** Hai

9. Determine the location of the Wen Chang and Wen Qu stars

The location of the Wen Chang and Wen Qu stars are based on the Birth Hour:

Si	Wu	Wei	Shen
Wen Qu Chen	**Zi Hour**		You
Mao			**Wen Chang** Xu
Yin	Chou	Zi	Hai

Wen Qu			
Si	Wu	Wei	Shen
Chen	**Chou Hour**		**Wen Chang** You
Mao			Xu
Yin	Chou	Zi	Hai

	Wen Qu		Wen Chang
Si	Wu	Wei	Shen
Chen	**Yin Hour**		You
Mao			Xu
Yin	Chou	Zi	Hai

		Wen Qu **Wen Chang**	
Si	Wu	Wei	Shen
Chen			You
Mao	**Mao Hour**		Xu
Yin	Chou	Zi	Hai

	Wen Chang		**Wen Qu**
Si	Wu	Wei	Shen
Chen			You
Mao	**Chen Hour**		Xu
Yin	Chou	Zi	Hai

Wen Chang Si	Wu	Wei	Shen
Chen			**Wen Qu** You
Mao	**Si Hour**		Xu
Yin	Chou	Zi	Hai

Si	Wu	Wei	Shen
Wen Chang Chen	**Wu Hour**		You
Mao			**Wen Qu** Xu
Yin	Chou	Zi	Hai

Si	Wu	Wei	Shen
Chen **Wen Chang** Mao	**Wei Hour**		You Xu
Yin	Chou	Zi	**Wen Qu** Hai

Si	Wu	Wei	Shen
Chen Mao	**Shen Hour**		You Xu
Wen Chang Yin	Chou	**Wen Qu** Zi	Hai

Si	Wu	Wei	Shen
Chen	**You Hour**		You
Mao			Xu
Yin	**Wen Qu** **Wen Chang** Chou	Zi	Hai

Si	Wu	Wei	Shen
Chen	**Xu Hour**		You
Mao			Xu
Wen Qu Yin	Chou	**Wen Chang** Zi	Hai

Si	Wu	Wei	Shen
Chen **Wen Qu** Mao	**Hai Hour**		You Xu
Yin	Chou	Zi	**Wen Chang** Hai

10. Determine the birth year Heavenly Stem Si Hua

Using your birth year Heavenly Stem, you can now determine the respective Si Hua:

Si Hua	Hua Lu	Hua Quan	Hua Ke	Hua Ji
Jia	Lian Zhen	Po Jun	Wu Qu	Tai Yang
Yi	Tian Ji	Tian Liang	Zi Wei	Tai Yin
Bing	Tian Tong	Tian Ji	Wen Chang	Lian Zhen
Ding	Tai Yin	Tian Tong	Tian Ji	Ju Men
Wu	Tan Lang	Tai Yin	You Bi	Tian Ji
Ji	Wu Qu	Tan Lang	Tian Liang	Wen Qu
Geng	Tai Yang	Wu Qu	Tai Yin	Tian Tong
Xin	Ju Men	Tai Yang	Wen Qu	Wen Chang
Ren	Tian Liang	Zi Wei	Zuo Fu	Wu Qu
Gui	Po Jun	Ju Men	Tai Yin	Tan Lang

11. Determine the Decade Cycle

The Decade Cycle is determined by the 5-Element and Yin Yang, starting from the Self Palace.

5-Element	Starting Age of Decade at Self Palace
2nd Water	2 – 11
3rd Wood	3 – 12
4th Metal	4 – 13
5th Earth	5 – 14
6th Fire	6 – 15

Gender	Decade Cycle
Yang Male	Clockwise
Yin Female	Clockwise
Yin Male	Anti-Clockwise
Yang Female	Anti-Clockwise

For example, a Male born on 6th Feb 2011 at 16:35, is Yin Male, 4th Metal element. So, the first Decade is 4-13, and it runs anti-clockwise.

Ju Men	Tian Xiang Lian Zhen	Tian Liang	Qi Sha
Gui 14-23 Si Siblings	Jia 4-13 Wu Self	Yi Wei Parents	Bing Shen Mental
Tan Lang **Zuo Fu**			**Tian Tong**
Ren 24-33 Chen Spouse	**6th Feb 2011 @16:35, Yin Male,** **4th Metal Element**		Ding 94-103 You Property
Tai Yin			**Wu Qu** **You Bi**
Xin 34-43 Mao Children			Wu 84-93 Xu Career
Zi Wei **Tian Fu** **Wen Chang**	**Tian Ji**	**Po Jun** **Wen Qu**	**Tai Yang**
Geng 44-53 Yin Wealth	Xin 54-63 Chou Health	Geng 64-73 Zi Travel	Ji 74-83 Hai Friends

Decade Chart

The Decade Chart is based on the 10 years decade cycle. For example, for the decade 14-23, it starts from the Si Palace and runs anti-clockwise:

Decade Self ▶ Decade Siblings ▶ Decade Spouse ▶ Decade Children ▶ Decade Wealth ▶ Decade Health ▶ Decade Travel ▶ Decade Friends ▶ Decade Career ▶ Decade Property ▶ Decade Mental ▶ Decade Parents.

Ju Men	Tian Xiang Lian Zhen	Tian Liang	Qi Sha
D.Self Gui 14-23 Si Siblings	*D.Parents* Jia 4-13 Wu Self	*D.Mental* Yi Wei Parents	*D.Property* Bing Shen Mental
Tan Lang **Zuo Fu** *D.Sibling* Ren 24-33 Chen Spouse	**6th Feb 2011 @16:35, Yin Male, 4th Metal Element**		**Tian Tong** *D.Career* Ding 94-103 You Property
Tai Yin *D.Spouse* Xin 34-43 Mao Children			**Wu Qu** **You Bi** *D.Friends* Wu 84-93 Xu Career
Zi Wei **Tian Fu** **Wen Chang** *D.Children* Geng 44-53 Yin Wealth	**Tian Ji** *D.Wealth* Xin 54-63 Chou Health	**Po Jun** **Wen Qu** *D.Health* Geng 64-73 Zi Travel	**Tai Yang** *D.Travel* Ji 74-83 Hai Friends

For reference, the decade chart for age 53-63 is as follow:

Ju Men	Tian Xiang Lian Zhen	Tian Liang	Qi Sha
D.Career Gui 14-23 Si Siblings	*D.Friends* Jia 4-13 Wu Self	*D.Travel* Yi Wei Parents	*D.Health* Bing Shen Mental
Tan Lang **Zuo Fu** D.Property Ren 24-33 Chen Spouse	**6th Feb 2011 @16:35, Yin Male, 4th Metal Element**		**Tian Tong** *D.Wealth* Ding 94-103 You Property
Tai Yin D.Mental Xin 34-43 Mao Children			**Wu Qu** **You Bi** *D.Children* Wu 84-93 Xu Career
Zi Wei **Tian Fu** **Wen Chang** *D.Parents* Geng 44-53 Yin Wealth	**Tian Ji** *D.Self* Xin 54-63 Chou Health	**Po Jun** **Wen Qu** *D.Siblings* Geng 64-73 Zi Travel	**Tai Yang** *D.Spouse* Ji 74-83 Hai Friends

12. Determine the Yearly Cycle

Using the Birth Year Heavenly Stem and Earthly Branch, locate it on the plotted chart. That is where the year cycle starts. For example, for a male born on 6th Feb 2011, the Birth Year is Xin Mao. So, 2011 starts at the Xin Mao Palace:

Ju Men	Tian Xiang Lian Zhen	Tian Liang	Qi Sha

2013 / 2025 Gui 14-23 Si Siblings	2014 / 2026 Jia 4-13 Wu Self	2015 / 2027 Yi Wei Parents	2016 / 2028 Bing Shen Mental
Tan Lang **Zuo Fu** 2012 / 2024 Ren 24-33 Chen Spouse	**6th Feb 2011 @16:35, Yin Male, 4th Metal Element**		**Tian Tong** 2017 / 2029 Ding 94-103 You Property
Tai Yin 2011 / 2023 Xin 34-43 Mao Children			**Wu Qu** **You Bi** 2018 / 2030 Wu 84-93 Xu Career
Zi Wei **Tian Fu** **Wen Chang** 2022 / 2034 Geng 44-53 Yin Wealth	**Tian Ji** 2021 / 2033 Xin 54-63 Chou Health	**Po Jun** **Wen Qu** 2020 / 2032 Geng 64-73 Zi Travel	**Tai Yang** 2019 / 2031 Ji 74-83 Hai Friends

13. Determine the Birth Year Si Hua

The Birth Year Si Hua is based on the year of birth with reference to the Si Hua chart. For example, on 6th Feb 2011 at 16:35, the birth year is Xin Mao:

Si Hua / Heavenly Stems	Hua Lu (化祿)	Hua Quan (化權)	Hua Ke (化科)	Hua Ji (化忌)
Xin	Ju Men	Tai Yang	Wen Qu	Wen Chang

Ju Men(祿)	Tian Xiang Lian Zhen	Tian Liang	Qi Sha

<table>
<tr>
<td>2013 / 2025
Gui   14-23
Si   Siblings</td>
<td>2014 / 2026
Jia   4-13
Wu   Self</td>
<td>2015 / 2027
Yi
Wei   Parents</td>
<td>2016 / 2028
Bing
Shen   Mental</td>
</tr>
<tr>
<td>Tan Lang
Zuo Fu

2012 / 2024
Ren   24-33
Chen   Spouse</td>
<td rowspan="2" colspan="2">6th Feb 2011 @16:35, Yin Male,
4th Metal Element</td>
<td>Tian Tong

2017 / 2029
Ding   94-103
You   Property</td>
</tr>
<tr>
<td>Tai Yin

2011 / 2023
Xin   34-43
Mao
Children</td>
<td>Wu Qu
You Bi

2018 / 2030
Wu   84-93
Xu   Career</td>
</tr>
<tr>
<td>Zi Wei
Tian Fu
Wen Chang(忌)
2022 / 2034
Geng   44-53
Yin   Wealth</td>
<td>Tian Ji

2021 / 2033
Xin   54-63
Chou
Health</td>
<td>Po Jun
Wen Qu(科)

2020 / 2032
Geng   64-73
Zi   Travel</td>
<td>Tai Yang(權)

2019 / 2031
Ji   74-83
Hai   Friends</td>
</tr>
</table>

14.   Determine the Self Si Hua

The Self Si Hua inspects the heavenly stem of an individual palace and maps it against the Si Hua chart. If the heavenly stem in a particular palace matches the star, then that star is the Self Si Hua star.

The Si Hua chart as follow:

Si Hua / Heavenly Stems	Hua Lu (化祿)	Hua Quan (化權)	Hua Ke (化科)	Hua Ji (化忌)
Jia	Lian Zhen	Po Jun	Wu Qu	Tai Yang
Yi	Tian Ji	Tian Liang	Zi Wei	Tai Yin
Bing	Tian Tong	Tian Ji	Wen Chang	Lian Zhen
Ding	Tai Yin	Tian Tong	Tian Ji	Ju Men
Wu	Tan Lang	Tai Yin	You Bi	Tian Ji
Ji	Wu Qu	Tan Lang	Tian Liang	Wen Qu
Geng	Tai Yang	Wu Qu	Tai Yin	Tian Tong
Xin	Ju Men	Tai Yang	Wen Qu	Wen Chang
Ren	Tian Liang	Zi Wei	Zuo Fu	Wu Qu
Gui	Po Jun	Ju Men	Tai Yin	Tan Lang

For example, at Si Palace, the Heavenly Stem is Gui. Gui Hua Quan at Ju Men and Ju Men is on the same palace. So, Ju Men star is Self Si Hua Quan.

<table>
<tr><td>Ju Men(祿)(權)

2013 / 2025
Gui   14-23
Si   Siblings</td></tr>
</table>

Ju Men(祿)(權) 2013 / 2025 Gui 14-23 Si Siblings	**Tian Xiang** **Lian Zhen(祿)** 2014 / 2026 Jia 4-13 Wu Self	**Tian Liang(權)** 2015 / 2027 Yi Wei Parents	**Qi Sha** 2016 / 2028 Bing Shen Mental
Tan Lang **Zuo Fu(科)** 2012 / 2024 Ren 24-33 Chen Spouse	**6th Feb 2011 @16:35, Yin Male, 4th Metal Element**		**Tian Tong(權)** 2017 / 2029 Ding 94-103 You Property
Tai Yin 2011 / 2023 Xin 34-43 Mao Children			**Wu Qu** **You Bi(科)** 2018 / 2030 Wu 84-93 Xu Career
Zi Wei **Tian Fu** **Wen Chang(忌)** 2022 / 2034 Geng 44-53 Yin Wealth	**Tian Ji** 2021 / 2033 Xin 54-63 Chou Health	**Po Jun** **Wen Qu(科)** 2020 / 2032 Geng 64-73 Zi Travel	**Tai Yang(權)** 2019 / 2031 Ji 74-83 Hai Friends

Note:

(祿): Birth Year Hua Lu

(權): Birth Year Hua Quan

(科): Birth Year Hua Ke

(忌): Birth Year Hua Ji

(祿): Self Hua Lu

(權): Self Hua Quan

(科): Self Hua Ke

(忌): Self Hua Ji

Part V – The Fine Dining

Some examples of how Zi Wei Dou Shu can be used in destiny analysis.

Methods of reading Zi Wei Dou Shu

There are various methods of reading Zi Wei Dou Shu and in this book, I will attempt to list down those that are most commonly used.

Natal chart Reading

The chart is plotted based on the person's birth date and time with all the Si Hua information indicated.

Character and attributes

Method 1:

The person's character is read from Self Palace against all the Stars in the palace:

- See *18 Stars of Zi Wei Dou Shu* for the attributes of each star.
- If there is Si Hua, then see the Si Hua attributes at: *Star Si Hua* at Palace:

Likewise, the person's other attributes can be read based on the Zi Wei Dou Shu 12 palaces. For example, Parents Palace stars tell the characteristics of how the person perceives his/her parents, in particular the person's father.

On the same manner, Wealth Palace shows how the person perceives his/her wealth. For example, People with Wu Qu (武曲) star at Wealth Palace will need to put in a lot of effort to make money (See Wu Qu at Wealth Palace). Although Wu Qu (武曲) star governs Wealth, but Wu Qu (武曲) star is an underground metal that requires refinement before it can be useful. As such, a person with Wu Qu (武曲) star at Wealth does not mean that the person will be wealthy. It just means that wealth is within reach but the person will need to work hard for it.

Method 2:

Using special Star Structure and Stars combo to read. See *Star Structure* and *Stars Combo* for more information.

Method 3:

Using the 6-Thread method to read. See 6-Threads Method (*六线法*).

Relationship Reading

Relationship reading means that we see the relationship of Zi Wei Dou Shu 12 palaces with each other. For example, what is the relationship between a person's Career Palace and the person?

Method 1:

Using the Natal Chart, see the Si Hua of that palace. For example, if Career Palace Si Hua Lu (化禄) to Self Palace, that means that for this person, he will have a good career for his whole life. Of course, whether or not this happens also depends on the Annual and Decade (Luck) cycle.

Method 2:

Similar to Method 1, the Palace Interchange method (宫位重叠) overlaps with the 6-thread method. For example, if a person's Career Palace Hua Ji and clash Career's Accident Thread, then this person is not suitable to work for people.

This method is also known as Master Kang's method, which is solely taught by Si Hua Grand Master, Kang Hui Huat.

Siblings	Self	Parents	Mental
Spouse	**Natal Chart**		Property
Children			Career
Wealth	Health	Travel	Friends

Siblings (Health)	Self (Wealth)	Parents (Children)	Mental (Spouse)
Spouse (Travel)	**Natal Chart inter use with Career**		Property (Siblings)
Children (Friends)			Career (Self)
Wealth (Career)	Health (Property)	Travel (Mental)	Friends (Parents)

- Career Hua Ji to Parents and clash Health.
- Parents/Health is Career's Children/Property or accident thread.

Method 3:

This method is also known as Master Kang's method, and it is called the 18 Flying Stars Method (十八四化非星). In this method, the stars fly based on the Si Hua Method and the resulting attributes are read. Due to the potency and accuracy of this method, details on how it works cannot be revealed by writing.

Decade Cycle Reading

Decade cycle reading is based on the following principal:

$$大限化给本命用，吉凶产生在流年$$

Meaning: Decade Chart Si Hua to Natal Chart, auspicious and inauspicious happens in Annual.

In a nutshell, Decade Chart (Body) Si Hua to Natal Chart (Use). When it happens, you have to see the Annual Chart. See *Inter Chart Si Hua* for more details.

Annual Cycle Reading

The Annual Chart is plotted based on the year earthly branch. For example, 1997 Annual Chart is as follows:

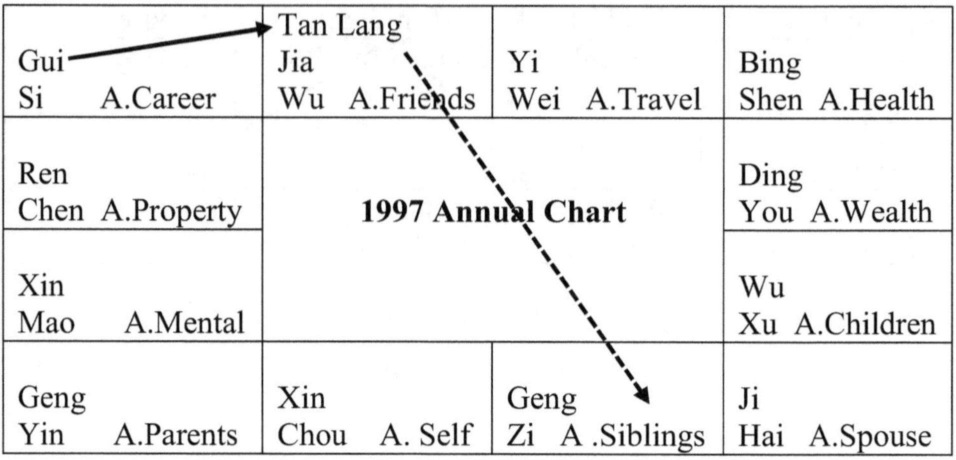

Gui Si A.Career	Tan Lang Jia Wu A.Friends	Yi Wei A.Travel	Bing Shen A.Health
Ren Chen A.Property	**1997 Annual Chart**		Ding You A.Wealth
Xin Mao A.Mental			Wu Xu A.Children
Geng Yin A.Parents	Xin Chou A. Self	Geng Zi A .Siblings	Ji Hai A.Spouse

Case 1: Lady Diana Spencer

Birthname Diana Frances Spencer
born on: 1 July 1961 at 19:45 (= 7:45 PM)
Place Sandringham, England, 52n50, 0e30
Timezone GDT h1e (is daylight saving time)

Natal Chart:

Tai Yin	Tan Lang You Bi	Tian Tong Ju Men(祿)	Wu Qu Tian Xiang Zuo Fu
Gui Si Children	Jia Wu Spouse	Yi Wei Siblings	Bing 6-15 Shen Self
Lian Zhen Tian Fu Ren 86-95 Chen Wealth	**1ˢᵗ July 1961 Xu Hour**		Tai Yang Tian Liang Ding 16-25 You Parents
Xin 76-85 Mao Health	**Yin Female, Fire 6**		Qi Sha Wu 26-35 Xu Mental
Po Jun Wen Qu(科) Geng 66-75 Yin Travel	Xin 56-65 Chou Friends	Zi Wei Wen Chang(忌) Geng 46-55 Zi Career	Tian Ji Ji 36-45 Hai Property

Character Reading

In mainstream Zi Wei Dou Shu, they will just interpret the characteristics of the stars in the palaces. For example, Self Palace has Wu Qu, Tian Xiang and Zuo Fu. So you can say that the person has the following characteristics:

- Wu Qu: People with Wu Qu (武曲) at Self Palace, they are calculative and because of that, they tend to be lonely. They are also stingy and will not want to spend money on themselves or on others.

- Tian Xiang: People with Tian Xiang (天相) at Self Palace do not have a very strong character. As such, their life will be more stable and have less changes. They will not take risks to improve themselves. They will prefer to keep to the conventional ways of doing things.

- Zuo Fu: People with Zuo Fu (左輔) at Self Palace are loyal, honest and sincere. Everyone will give him/her respect.

The same can be applied to each palace (e.g. Spouse, Children, Career etc). This is similar to the San He method of reading, where the characteristics of the stars are read against the palaces.

The true Si Hua method of reading is as follow:

Self Palace represents the person. Using the Self Palace as a reference, you look at which palace the Si Hua lands on. For example, in Lady Diana's chart, the Self Palace is Bing. The Si Hua information is as follows:

Si Hua	Hua Lu	Hua Quan	Hua Ke	Hua Ji
Bing	Tian Tong	Tian Ji	Wen Chang	Lian Zhen

In her Self Palace, Bing Hua Lu to the Siblings Palace. Hua Lu refers to something that you want and are most concerned about. That means that she is most concerned about her siblings. In addition, Siblings Palace also represents her mother. Lady Diana's parents divorced when she was seven. She and her brother stayed with her father after a bitter custody battle. Thus, having a mother might be something she longed for.

Her Self Palace Bing, Hua Ji to Wealth Palace. Hua Ji refers to something you regret or something that you cannot get. Please note that you can use Palace Interchange for further reading. For example, Wealth Palace is Spouse's Spouse, which refers to Prince Charles's Spouse, which is Lady Camilla, Duchess of Cornwall. So, her biggest regret is Lady Camilla, who destroyed her marriage.

The same concept can be used for other palaces as well. For example:

Tai Yin Gui Si Children	Tan Lang You Bi Jia Wu Spouse	Tian Tong Ju Men(祿) Yi Wei Siblings	Wu Qu Tian Xiang Zuo Fu Bing 6-15 Shen Self
Lian Zhen Tian Fu Ren 86-95 Chen Wealth	**1ˢᵗ July 1961 Xu Hour Yin Female, Fire 6**		Tai Yang Tian Liang Ding 16-25 You Parents
  Xin 76-85 Mao Health			Qi Sha Wu 26-35 Xu Mental
Po Jun Wen Qu(科) Geng 66-75 Yin Travel	Xin 56-65 Chou Friends	Zi Wei Wen Chang(忌) Geng 46-55 Zi Career	Tian Ji Ji 36-45 Hai Property

Spouse Hua Ji to Parents and clash Health. That also means that Spouse Hua Ji to Parents-Health Thread, which happen to Spouse's Children-Property Thread or Spouse's accident thread. Normally, for charts like this, there is high chance for the person to get divorced, but whether or not it will actually happen will depend on other factors.

Tai Yin Gui Si Children	Tan Lang You Bi Jia Wu Spouse	Tian Tong Ju Men(祿) Yi Wei Siblings	Wu Qu Tian Xiang Zuo Fu Bing 6-15 Shen Self
Lian Zhen Tian Fu Ren 86-95 Chen Wealth	**1ˢᵗ July 1961 Xu Hour Yin Female, Fire 6**		Tai Yang Tian Liang Ding 16-25 You Parents
Xin 76-85 Mao Health			Qi Sha Wu 26-35 Xu Mental
Po Jun Wen Qu(科) Geng 66-75 Yin Travel	Xin 56-65 Chou Friends	Zi Wei Wen Chang(忌) Geng 46-55 Zi Career	Tian Ji Ji 36-45 Hai Property

The Siblings Palace also represents her mother. This is because the Parents Palace mainly refers to her father. So, the Parents Palace's Spouse is the Natal Chart Siblings Palace, which represents her mother.

Siblings Palace Hua Ji clashes her Children-Property Thread. That means that her mother does not have any affinity with her.

Event Reading

In November 1980 (Geng Shen year), she met Prince Charles, whom she had already idolized. After five months of engagement, they were married at St. Paul's Cathedral on 29ᵗʰ July 1981 (Xin You year).

For an event reading, it has to be initiated from Decade Chart to Natal Chart overlapping with Annual Chart.

Her 16-25 decade chart is as follow:

<table>
<tr>
<td>Tai Yin

D.Wealth
Gui
Si Children</td>
<td>Tan Lang
You Bi

D.Children
Jia
Wu Spouse</td>
<td>Tian Tong
Ju Men(祿)

D.Spouse
Yi
Wei Siblings</td>
<td>Wu Qu
Tian Xiang
Zuo Fu

D.Siblings
Bing   6-15
Shen   Self</td>
</tr>
<tr>
<td>Lian Zhen
Tian Fu

D.Health
Ren 86-95
Chen Wealth</td>
<td colspan="2" rowspan="2" align="center">1st July 1961 Xu Hour
Yin Female, Fire 6

16-25 Decade</td>
<td>Tai Yang
Tian Liang

D.Self
Ding 16-25
You Parents</td>
</tr>
<tr>
<td>
D.Travel
Xin 76-85
Mao Health</td>
<td>Qi Sha

D.Parents
Wu 26-35
Xu Mental</td>
</tr>
<tr>
<td>Po Jun
Wen Qu(科)

D.Friends
Geng 66-75
Yin Travel</td>
<td>
D.Career
Xin 56-65
Chou Friends</td>
<td>Zi Wei
Wen Chang(忌)

D.Property
Geng 46-55
Zi Career</td>
<td>Tian Ji

D.Mental
Ji 36-45
Hai Property</td>
</tr>
</table>

Si Hua / Heavenly Stems	Hua Lu (化祿)	Hua Quan (化權)	Hua Ke (化科)	Hua Ji (化忌)
Geng	Tai Yang	Wu Qu	Tai Yin	Tian Tong

Decade Friends Palace Hua Lu to Natal Parents Palace. Friends = Boyfriend or someone who you want to marry, and this Hua Lu to Parents Palace. Parents Palace is also Spouse's Property. Thus, the chart shows a friend moving to the spouse's house, which represents getting married.

The Annual chart is as follow:

Tai Yin A.Wealth Gui Si Children	**Tan Lang** **You Bi** A.Children Jia Wu Spouse	**Tian Tong** **Ju Men**(祿) A.Spouse Yi Wei Siblings	**Wu Qu** **Tian Xiang** **Zuo Fu** A.Siblings Bing 6-15 Shen Self
Lian Zhen **Tian Fu** A.Health Ren 86-95 Chen Wealth	**1st July 1961 Xu Hour** **Yin Female, Fire 6** **1981 Annual Chart.**		**Tai Yang** **Tian Liang** A.Self Ding 16-25 You Parents
A.Travel Xin 76-85 Mao Health			**Qi Sha** A.Parents Wu 26-35 Xu Mental
Po Jun **Wen Qu**(科) A.Friends Geng 66-75 Yin Travel	A.Career Xin 56-65 Chou Friends	**Zi Wei** **Wen Chang**(忌) A.Property Geng 46-55 Zi Career	**Tian Ji** A.Mental Ji 36-45 Hai Property

The Annual chart overlaps with the Decade chart and hence the event happened.

Lady Diana and Prince Charles divorced in July 1996.

Tai Yin D.Health Gui Si Children	Tan Lang You Bi D.Wealth Jia Wu Spouse	Tian Tong Ju Men(祿) D.Children Yi Wei Siblings	Wu Qu Tian Xiang Zuo Fu D.Spouse Bing 6-15 Shen Self
Lian Zhen Tian Fu D.Travel Ren 86-95 Chen Wealth			Tai Yang Tian Liang D.Siblings Ding 16-25 You Parents
	1st July 1961 Xu Hour		
			Qi Sha D.Self Wu 26-35 Xu Mental
D.Friends Xin 76-85 Mao Health			
Po Jun Wen Qu(科) D.Career Geng 66-75 Yin Travel	 D.Property Xin 56-65 Chou Friends	Zi Wei Wen Chang(忌) D.Mental Geng 46-55 Zi Career	Tian Ji D.Parents Ji 36-45 Hai Property

As mentioned above, her natal chart already shows that there will be problems with her relationship(s). During 26-35 Decade, her Decade Wealth overlap with her Natal Spouse Palace and clashes her Spouse's Children-Property Thread. Decade Wealth is also the Decade Spouse's Spouse. So, a Spouse's Spouse (e.g. Husband's mistress) will come to destroy the relationship.

This happened in 1996 when the Annual chart overlapped with the Decade and Natal chart:

Tai Yin A.Health Gui Si Children	Tan Lang You Bi A.Wealth Jia Wu Spouse	Tian Tong Ju Men(禄) A.Children Yi Wei Siblings	Wu Qu Tian Xiang Zuo Fu A.Spouse Bing 6-15 Shen Self
Lian Zhen Tian Fu A.Travel Ren 86-95 Chen Wealth	**1ˢᵗ July 1961 Xu Hour** **Yin Female, Fire 6** **1996 Chart**		Tai Yang Tian Liang A.Siblings Ding 16-25 You Parents
A.Friends Xin 76-85 Mao Health			Qi Sha A.Self Wu 26-35 Xu Mental
Po Jun Wen Qu(科) A.Career Geng 66-75 Yin Travel	A.Property Xin 56-65 Chou Friends	Zi Wei Wen Chang(忌) A.Mental Geng 46-55 Zi Career	Tian Ji A.Parents Ji 36-45 Hai Property

Lady Diana and Dodi died in a car accident in a tunnel along the river Seine in Paris on 31st August 1997.

Tai Yin D.Travel Gui Si Children	Tan Lang You Bi D.Health Jia Wu Spouse	Tian Tong Ju Men(禄) D.Wealth Yi Wei Siblings	Wu Qu Tian Xiang Zuo Fu D.Children Bing 6-15 Shen Self
Lian Zhen Tian Fu D.Friends Ren 86-95 Chen Wealth	1st July 1961 Xu Hour Yin Female, Fire 6 36-45 Decade		Tai Yang Tian Liang D.Spouse Ding 16-25 You Parents
D.Career Xin 76-85 Mao Health			Qi Sha D.Siblings Wu 26-35 Xu Mental
Po Jun Wen Qu(科) D.Property Geng 66-75 Yin Travel	D.Mental Xin 56-65 Chou Friends	Zi Wei Wen Chang(忌) D.Parents Geng 46-55 Zi Career	Tian Ji D.Self Ji 36-45 Hai Property

A car accident is related to travel, so the accident has to be triggered from Decade Travel. Her Decade Travel Hua Ji to her Spouse-Career thread, which happens to be her Health's Children-Property thread. Health's accident thread means that she will get injured from the accident.

Case 2: Michael Jordan

Birthname: Michael Jeffrey Jordan
born on: 17 February 1963 at 10:20 (= 10:20 AM)
Place: Brooklyn NY, USA, 40n38, 73w56
Timezone: EST h5w (is standard time)

Natal Chart:

<table>
<tr>
<td>Wu Qu
Po Jun(祿)
Wen Chang

Ding   43-52
Si   Wealth</td>
<td>Tai Yang

Wu   33-42
Wu   Children</td>
<td>Tian Fu

Ji   23-32
Wei   Spouse</td>
<td>Tian Ji
Tai Yin(科)

Geng   13-22
Shen   Siblings</td>
</tr>
<tr>
<td>Tian Tong(祿)
Zuo Fu

Bing   53-62
Chen   Health</td>
<td colspan="2" rowspan="2">17th Feb 1963 Si Hour
Yin Male, Wood 3</td>
<td>Zi Wei
Tan Lang(忌)
Wen Qu

Xin
You   Self</td>
</tr>
<tr>
<td>
Yi   63-72
Mao   Travel</td>
<td>Ju Men(權)
You Bi

Ren
Xu   Parents</td>
</tr>
<tr>
<td>
Jia   73-82
Yin   Friends</td>
<td>Qi Sha
Lian Zhen

Yi
Chou   Career</td>
<td>Tian Liang

Jia
Zi   Property</td>
<td>Tian Xiang

Gui
Hai   Mental</td>
</tr>
</table>

Michael Jeffrey Jordan (born February 17, 1963), also known by his initials, MJ, is an American former professional basketball player, entrepreneur, and majority owner and chairman of the Charlotte Bobcats. His biography on the National Basketball Association (NBA) website states, "By acclamation, Michael Jordan is the greatest basketball player of all time." Jordan was one of the most effectively marketed athletes of his generation and was considered instrumental in popularizing the NBA around the world in the 1980s and 1990s[2].

Natal Chart Reading

Michael Jordon made a lot of money from his basketball career. From his chart:

<table>
<tr>
<td>

Wu Qu
Po Jun(祿)
Wen Chang

Ding   43-52
Si   Wealth
</td>
<td>

Tai Yang

Wu   33-42
Wu   Children
</td>
<td>

Tian Fu

Ji   23-32
Wei   Spouse
</td>
<td>

Tian Ji
Tai Yin(科)

Geng   13-22
Shen   Siblings
</td>
</tr>
<tr>
<td>

Tian Tong(祿)
Zuo Fu

Bing   53-62
Chen   Health
</td>
<td colspan="2" rowspan="2">

17th Feb 1963 Si Hour
Yin Male, Wood 3
</td>
<td>

Zi Wei
Tan Lang(忌)
Wen Qu

Xin
You   Self
</td>
</tr>
<tr>
<td>

Yi   63-72
Mao   Travel
</td>
<td>

Ju Men(權)
You Bi

Ren
Xu   Parents
</td>
</tr>
<tr>
<td>

Jia   73-82
Yin   Friends
</td>
<td>

Qi Sha
Lian Zhen

Yi
Chou   Career
</td>
<td>

Tian Liang

Jia
Zi   Property
</td>
<td>

Tian Xiang

Gui
Hai   Mental
</td>
</tr>
</table>

His Career Palace, Yi Tian Ji Hua Lu to his Siblings Palace. His Siblings Palace is also his Wealth's Property. That means his Career contributes to his Wealth's Property. Tian Ji star also means

---

[2] From Wikipedia

movement. That means that he needs to have a lot of movement in his career. Thus, a basketball career was a good decision for him. When he switched to baseball, there was less movement as compared to basketball, which is why he was not as successful.

In addition, Siblings also means his teammate. So, by working with his teammates, he will be successful.

Wu Qu **Po Jun**(祿) **Wen Chang** Ding 43-52 Si Wealth	**Tai Yang** Wu 33-42 Wu Children	**Tian Fu** Ji 23-32 Wei Spouse	**Tian Ji** **Tai Yin**(科) Geng 13-22 Shen Siblings
Tian Tong(祿) **Zuo Fu** Bing 53-62 Chen Health	**17th Feb 1963 Si Hour** **Yin Male, Wood 3**		**Zi Wei** **Tan Lang**(忌) **Wen Qu** Xin You Self
Yi 63-72 Mao Travel			**Ju Men**(權) **You Bi** Ren Xu Parents
Jia 73-82 Yin Friends	**Qi Sha** **Lian Zhen** Yi Chou Career	**Tian Liang** Jia Zi Property	**Tian Xiang** Gui Hai Mental

In addition, his Wealth Palace Ding Tai Yin Hua Lu to his Siblings Palace as well. That means that his Wealth Hua Lu to his Wealth's Property as well.

Event Reading
From Wikipedia:

In 1991, he won his first NBA championship with the Bulls, and followed that achievement with titles in 1992 and 1993, securing a "three-peat". Although Jordan abruptly retired from basketball at the beginning of the 1993–94 NBA season to pursue a career in baseball, he rejoined the Bulls in 1995 and led them to three additional championships (1996, 1997, and 1998) as well as an NBA-record 72 regular-season wins in the 1995–96 NBA season. Jordan retired for a second time in 1999, but returned for two more NBA seasons from 2001 to 2003 as a member of the Washington Wizards.

His successful career span over 2 of his Decade luck, 23-32 & 33-42.

Decade 23-32:

Wu Qu Po Jun(禄) Wen Chang D.Spouse Ding　43-52 Si　Wealth	Tai Yang D.Siblings Wu　33-42 Wu　Children	Tian Fu D.Self Ji　23-32 Wei　Spouse	Tian Ji Tai Yin(科) D.Parents Geng　13-22 Shen　Siblings
Tian Tong(禄) Zuo Fu D.Children Bing　53-62 Chen　Health		17ᵗʰ Feb 1963 Si Hour Yin Male, Wood 3	Zi Wei Tan Lang(忌) Wen Qu D.Mental Xin You　Self
  D.Wealth Yi　63-72 Mao　Travel			Ju Men(權) You Bi D.Property Ren Xu　Parents
 D.Health Jia　73-82 Yin　Friends	Qi Sha Lian Zhen D.Travel Yi Chou　Career	Tian Liang D.Friends Jia Zi　Property	Tian Xiang D.Career Gui Hai　Mental

Decade Career is at his Hai Palace, Gui Po Jun Hua Lu to Wealth. That means, his Decade Career Hua Lu to his Natal Wealth Palace, and he makes money from his Career.

In addition, his Decade Wealth is at Mao Palace, Yi Tian Ji Hua Lu to his Siblings Palace, which is his Wealth's Property. That means his Wealth goes to his Wealth's Property, and all his money is stored up.

Decade 33-42:

<table>
<tr>
<td>

Wu Qu
Po Jun(祿)
Wen Chang

D.Siblings
Ding   43-52
Si   Wealth
</td>
<td>

Tai Yang

D.Self
Wu   33-42
Wu   Children
</td>
<td>

Tian Fu

D.Parents
Ji   23-32
Wei Spouse
</td>
<td>

Tian Ji
Tai Yin(科)

D.Mental
Geng 13-22
Shen Siblings
</td>
</tr>
<tr>
<td>

Tian Tong(祿)
Zuo Fu

D.Spouse
Bing 53-62
Chen Health
</td>
<td colspan="2" rowspan="2">

17th Feb 1963 Si Hour
Yin Male, Wood 3
</td>
<td>

Zi Wei
Tan Lang(忌)
Wen Qu

D.Property
Xin
You   Self
</td>
</tr>
<tr>
<td>

D.Children
Yi   63-72
Mao Travel
</td>
<td>

Ju Men(權)
You Bi

D.Career
Ren
Xu   Parents
</td>
</tr>
<tr>
<td>

D.Wealth
Jia   73-82
Yin Friends
</td>
<td>

Qi Sha
Lian Zhen

D.Health
Yi
Chou Career
</td>
<td>

Tian Liang

D.Travel
Jia
Zi   Property
</td>
<td>

Tian Xiang

D.Friends
Gui
Hai Mental
</td>
</tr>
</table>

Decade Career is at Xu Palace, Ren Hua Lu Tian Liang to Property. Property is also Wealth's Health, which also means savings. So, his career will contribute to his savings.

In addition, Decade Wealth is at Yin Palace, Jia Hua Lu Lian Zhen at Career Palace. Wealth is supporting his Career, so will he continue to make money in this decade.

He married Juanita Vanoy in September 1989 but his son was born in Nov 1988.

Wu Qu Po Jun(禄) Wen Chang D.Spouse Ding 43-52 Si Wealth	Tai Yang D.Siblings Wu 33-42 Wu Children	Tian Fu D.Self Ji 23-32 Wei Spouse	Tian Ji Tai Yin(科) D.Parents Geng 13-22 Shen Siblings
Tian Tong(禄) Zuo Fu D.Children Bing 53-62 Chen Health	17th Feb 1963 Si Hour Yin Male, Wood 3		Zi Wei Tan Lang(忌) Wen Qu D.Mental Xin You Self
D.Wealth Yi 63-72 Mao Travel			Ju Men(權) You Bi D.Property Ren Xu Parents
D.Health Jia 73-82 Yin Friends	Qi Sha Lian Zhen D.Travel Yi Chou Career	Tian Liang D.Friends Jia Zi Property	Tian Xiang D.Career Gui Hai Mental

His Decade Spouse Ding Hua Ji Ju Men at his Parents Palace (Spouse's Property) and clash his Health Palace. That means that his

Spouse is coming to clash him, which also means that he will get married.

In addition, his Decade Spouse Ding Hua Quan Tian Tong to his Health Palace. Hua Quan means authority, Tian Tong means Children. His Health Palace also represents Spouse's Children. So, he married her because she gave birth to his son.

1989 is at Si Palace:

Wu Qu **Po Jun**(禄) **Wen Chang** A.Self Ding 43-52 Si Wealth	**Tai Yang** A.Parents Wu 33-42 Wu Children	**Tian Fu** A.Mental Ji 23-32 Wei Spouse	**Tian Ji** **Tai Yin**(科) A.Property Geng 13-22 Shen Siblings
Tian Tong(禄) **Zuo Fu** A.Siblings Bing 53-62 Chen Health	**17th Feb 1963 Si Hour** **Yin Male, Wood 3** **1989 Annual Chart**		**Zi Wei** **Tan Lang**(忌) **Wen Qu** A.Career Xin You Self
A.Spouse Yi 63-72 Mao Travel			**Ju Men**(權) **You Bi** A.Friends Ren Xu Parents
A.Children Jia 73-82 Yin Friends	**Qi Sha** **Lian Zhen** A.Wealth Yi Chou Career	**Tian Liang** A.Health Jia Zi Property	**Tian Xiang** A.Travel Gui Hai Mental

Case 3: Angelina Jolie

Birthname Angelina Jolie Voight
born on: 4 June 1975 at 09:09 (= 09:09 AM)
Place Los Angeles, California, 34n03, 118w15
Timezone PDT h7w (is daylight saving time)

Natal Chart

<table>
<tr>
<td>Lian Zhen
Tan Lang
Wen Chang(忌)

Xin   56-65
Si   Friends</td>
<td>Ju Men

Ren   66-75
Wu   Travel</td>
<td>Tian Xiang
Zuo Fu
You Bi

Gui
Wei   Health</td>
<td>Tian Tong
Tian Liang(權)

Jia
Shen   Wealth</td>
</tr>
<tr>
<td>Tai Yin(忌)

Geng   46-55
Chen   Career</td>
<td rowspan="2" colspan="2" align="center">4th June 1975 Si Hour
Yin Female, Fire 6</td>
<td>Wu Qu
Qi Sha
Wen Qu

Yi
You   Children</td>
</tr>
<tr>
<td>Tian Fu

Ji   36-45
Mao   Property</td>
<td>Tai Yang

Bing
Xu   Spouse</td>
</tr>
<tr>
<td>
Wu   26-35
Yin   Mental</td>
<td>Zi Wei(科)
Po Jun

Ji   16-25
Chou   Parents</td>
<td>Tian Ji (祿忌)

Wu   6-15
Zi   Self</td>
<td>
Ding
Hai   Siblings</td>
</tr>
</table>

From Wikipedia:

Born in Los Angeles, California, Jolie is the daughter of actors Jon Voight and Marcheline Bertrand. After her parents' separation in 1976, Jolie and her brother lived with their mother, who had abandoned her acting ambitions to focus on raising her children

From her natal chart, it shows that she has bad affinity with her father:

Lian Zhen **Tan Lang** **Wen Chang**(忌) Xin 56-65 Si Friends	**Ju Men** Ren 66-75 Wu Travel	**Tian Xiang** **Zuo Fu** **You Bi** Gui Wei Health	**Tian Tong** **Tian Liang**(權) Jia Shen Wealth
Tai Yin(忌) Geng 46-55 Chen Career	**4ᵗʰ June 1975 Si Hour**	**Yin Female, Fire 6**	**Wu Qu** **Qi Sha** **Wen Qu** Yi You Children
Tian Fu Ji 36-45 Mao Property			**Tai Yang** Bing Xu Spouse
  Wu 26-35 Yin Mental	**Zi Wei**(科) **Po Jun** Ji 16-25 Chou Parents	**Tian Ji** (祿忌) Wu 6-15 Zi Self	**Ding** Ding Hai Siblings

Ji at Parents Palace Wen Qu Hua Ji and clash her Accident Thread. This shows that she lacks affinity with her father.

She was known to have adopted a few children. From Wikipedia:

On March 10, 2002, Jolie adopted her first child, seven-month-old Maddox Chivan, from an orphanage in Battambang, Cambodia. He was born as Rath Vibol on August 5, 2001, in a local village.

Jolie adopted a daughter, six-month-old Zahara Marley, from an orphanage in Addis Ababa, Ethiopia, on July 6, 2005.

On March 15, 2007, Jolie adopted a son, three-year-old Pax Thien, from an orphanage in Ho Chi Minh City, Vietnam

To see adoption in Zi Wei Dou Shu, we have to think logically. Basically, for adoption, it is normally seen from Friend's Children. Using the inter-palace method, Friend's Children = Mental Palace. During her 26-35 Decade:

Lian Zhen **Tan Lang** **Wen Chang**(忌) D.Property Xin 56-65 Si Friends	**Ju Men** D.Career Ren 66-75 Wu Travel	**Tian Xiang** **Zuo Fu** **You Bi** D.Friends Gui Wei Health	**Tian Tong** **Tian Liang**(權) D.Travel Jia Shen Wealth
Tai Yin(忌) D. Mental Geng 46-55 Chen Career		**4th June 1975 Si Hour** **Yin Female, Fire 6**	**Wu Qu** **Qi Sha** **Wen Qu** D.Health Yi You Children
Tian Fu D.Parents Ji 36-45 Mao Property			**Tai Yang** D.Wealth Bing Xu Spouse
D.Self Wu 26-35 Yin Mental	**Zi Wei**(科) **Po Jun** D.Siblings Ji 16-25 Chou Parents	**Tian Ji** (祿忌) D.Spouse Wu 6-15 Zi Self	**D.Children** Ding Hai Siblings

Geng Wu Qu Hua Quan: Decade Mental Hua Quan to Children Palace. Decade Mental = Decade Friend's Children. Hua Quan represents passing the authority over, so the authority is passed over to the Children Palace. Therefore, it means that she took her Friend's Children as her own Children, which refers to adoption.

She started to make a lot of money during her 26-35 Decade:

Decade 26-35:

Lian Zhen **Tan Lang** **Wen Chang**(忌) D.Property Xin 56-65 Si Friends	**Ju Men** D.Career Ren 66-75 Wu Travel	**Tian Xiang** **Zuo Fu** **You Bi** D.Friends Gui Wei Health	**Tian Tong** **Tian Liang**(權) D.Travel Jia Shen Wealth
Tai Yin(忌) D. Mental Geng 46-55 Chen Career	**4th June 1975 Si Hour** **Yin Female, Fire 6**		**Wu Qu** **Qi Sha** **Wen Qu** D.Health Yi You Children
Tian Fu D.Parents Ji 36-45 Mao Property			**Tai Yang** D.Wealth Bing Xu Spouse
  D.Self Wu 26-35 Yin Mental	**Zi Wei**(科) **Po Jun** D.Siblings Ji 16-25 Chou Parents	**Tian Ji** (祿忌) D.Spouse Wu 6-15 Zi Self	**Tian Yang** D.Children Ding Hai Siblings

Decade Career Ren Hua Lu Tian Liang to her Wealth Palace. In addition, her Decade Wealth Bing, Hua Lu to her Wealth Palace as well.

Although she is very successful, she does not seems to have luck in her relationships. This can be seen from her natal chart:

Lian Zhen **Tan Lang** **Wen Chang**(忌) Xin 56-65 Si Friends	**Ju Men** Ren 66-75 Wu Travel	**Tian Xiang** **Zuo Fu** **You Bi** Gui Wei Health	**Tian Tong** **Tian Liang**(權) Jia Shen Wealth
Tai Yin(忌) Geng 46-55 Chen Career	**4th June 1975 Si Hour** **Yin Female, Fire 6**		**Wu Qu** **Qi Sha** **Wen Qu** Yi You Children
Tian Fu Ji 36-45 Mao Property			**Tai Yang** Bing Xu Spouse
  Wu 26-35 Yin Mental	**Zi Wei**(科) **Po Jun** Ji 16-25 Chou Parents	**Tian Ji** (祿忌) Wu 6-15 Zi Self	 Ding Hai Siblings

Bing at Spouse Palace, Hua Ji Lian Zhen and clash Friends/Siblings thread. Friends/Siblings thread is known as the achievement thread. So, there is no achievement in her relationships. Here is a list of her romantic relationships:

- Jolie had a serious boyfriend for two years from the age of 14.

- During the filming of Hackers (1995), Jolie had a romantic relationship with British actor Jonny Lee Miller, her first lover since the relationship in her early teens. They were not in touch for many months after production ended, but eventually reconnected and married soon after in March 1996. Their divorce, initiated by Jolie in February 1999, was finalized shortly before she remarried the next year.
- Prior to her marriage to Miller, Jolie began a relationship with model-actress Jenny Shimizu
- After a two-month courtship, Jolie married actor Billy Bob Thornton on May 5, 2000
- Jolie was involved in a well-publicized Hollywood scandal when she was accused of having caused the 2005 divorce of actors Brad Pitt and Jennifer Aniston. Jolie and Pitt married on August 23, 2014. After two years of marriage, the couple separated in September 2016

Case 4: Robert Downey Jr.

Birthname: Robert John Downey, Jr
born on: 4 April 1965 at 13:10 (= 1:10 PM)
Place: Manhattan, New York, 40n46, 73w59
Timezone: EST h5w (is standard time)

Natal Chart:

<table>
<tr>
<td>Ju Men(祿)

Xin 42-51
Si   Wealth</td>
<td>Tian Xiang
Lian Zhen
Zuo Fu

Ren 32-41
Wu   Children</td>
<td>Tian Liang(權)

Gui 22-31
Wei   Spouse</td>
<td>Qi Sha
You Bi

Jia 12-21
Shen   Siblings</td>
</tr>
<tr>
<td>Tan Lang

Geng 52-61
Chen Health</td>
<td rowspan="2" colspan="2" align="center">4th April 1965 Wei Hour
Yin Male, Water 2</td>
<td>Tian Tong

Yi
You   Self</td>
</tr>
<tr>
<td>Tai Yin(忌)
Wen Chang

Ji 62-71
Mao Travel</td>
<td>Wu Qu

Bing
Xu   Parents</td>
</tr>
<tr>
<td>Zi Wei(科)
Tian Fu

Wu 72-81
Yin   Friends</td>
<td>Tian Ji(祿)

Ji
Chou Career</td>
<td>Po Jun

Wu
Zi   Property</td>
<td>Tai Yang
Wen Qu

Ding
Hai   Mental</td>
</tr>
</table>

Robert Downey Jr. is an American actor that is famous for playing the character Iron Man. Between 1996 to 2001, he has been in and out of prison due to drug abuse:

- Arrest June 1996 (Stopped for speeding, found drugs)
- Institutionalized - prison, hospital 20 July 1996 (Drugs)
- Arrest 8 December 1997 (Returned to jail for parole violation)
- Assault/ Battery Perpetration 13 February 1998 (Fight with another jail inmate)
- Institutionalized - prison, hospital 22 June 1999 at 12:00 midnight in Los Angeles, CA (L.A. County Jail rehab)
- Trial dates 5 August 1999 at 12:00 noon in Los Angeles, CA (Sentenced to two years in prison)
- Arrest 24 April 2001 (Drug arrest)

All these happened during his Decade: 32-41.

Ju Men(祿)	**Tian Xiang** **Lian Zhen** **Zuo Fu**	**Tian Liang**(權)	**Qi Sha** **You Bi**
D.Siblings Xin 42-51 Si Wealth	D.Self Ren 32-41 Wu Children	D.Parents Gui 22-31 Wei Spouse	D.Mental Jia 12-21 Shen Siblings
Tan Lang D.Spouse Geng 52-61 Chen Health	4th April 1965 Wei Hour	Yin Male, Water 2	**Tian Tong** D.Property Yi You Self
Tai Yin(忌) **Wen Chang** D.Children Ji 62-71 Mao Travel			**Wu Qu** D.Career Bing Xu Parents
Zi Wei(科) **Tian Fu** D.Wealth Wu 72-81 Yin Friends	**Tian Ji**(祿) D.Health Ji Chou Career	**Po Jun** D.Travel Wu Zi Property	**Tai Yang** **Wen Qu** D.Friends Ding Hai Mental

Gui Hua Ji Tan Lang and clash Parents. Therefore, Decade Parents clash Parents Palace. Parents Palace represents authority. Decade Authority coming to clash Authority, which means that he will get into trouble.

On 21 January 2001, he was awarded a Golden Globe as Best Supporting actor in a TV series, Ally McBeal.

Ju Men(祿) D.Siblings Xin 42-51 Si Wealth	Tian Xiang Lian Zhen Zuo Fu D.Self Ren 32-41 Wu Children	Tian Liang(權) D.Parents Gui 22-31 Wei Spouse	Qi Sha You Bi D.Mental Jia 12-21 Shen Siblings
Tan Lang D.Spouse Geng 52-61 Chen Health			Tian Tong D.Property Yi You Self
Tai Yin(忌) Wen Chang D.Children Ji 62-71 Mao Travel	**4th April 1965 Wei Hour Yin Male, Water 2**		Wu Qu D.Career Bing Xu Parents
Zi Wei(科) Tian Fu D.Wealth Wu 72-81 Yin Friends	Tian Ji(祿) D.Health Ji Chou Career	Po Jun D.Travel Wu Zi Property	Tai Yang Wen Qu D.Friends Ding Hai Mental

His fans are represented by the Children Palace. His Decade Children Hua Lu Wu Qu to his Parents/Health Thread, which is his brightness thread. Thus, he started becoming famous during this time.

Appendix

Date	Lunar	Leap Mth		Date	Lunar	Leap Mth
1950-02-17	1950-01-01	No		1953-09-08	1953-08-01	No
1950-03-18	1950-02-01	No		1953-10-08	1953-09-01	No
1950-04-17	1950-03-01	No		1953-11-07	1953-10-01	No
1950-05-17	1950-04-01	No		1953-12-06	1953-11-01	No
1950-06-15	1950-05-01	No		1954-01-05	1953-12-01	No
1950-07-15	1950-06-01	No		1954-02-03	1954-01-01	No
1950-08-14	1950-07-01	No		1954-03-05	1954-02-01	No
1950-09-12	1950-08-01	No		1954-04-03	1954-03-01	No
1950-10-11	1950-09-01	No		1954-05-03	1954-04-01	No
1950-11-10	1950-10-01	No		1954-06-01	1954-05-01	No
1950-12-09	1950-11-01	No		1954-06-30	1954-06-01	No
1951-01-08	1950-12-01	No		1954-07-30	1954-07-01	No
1951-02-06	1951-01-01	No		1954-08-28	1954-08-01	No
1951-03-08	1951-02-01	No		1954-09-27	1954-09-01	No
1951-04-06	1951-03-01	No		1954-10-27	1954-10-01	No
1951-05-06	1951-04-01	No		1954-11-25	1954-11-01	No
1951-06-05	1951-05-01	No		1954-12-25	1954-12-01	No
1951-07-04	1951-06-01	No		1955-01-24	1955-01-01	No
1951-08-03	1951-07-01	No		1955-02-22	1955-02-01	No
1951-09-01	1951-08-01	No		1955-03-24	1955-03-01	No
1951-10-01	1951-09-01	No		1955-04-22	1955-03-01	Yes
1951-10-30	1951-10-01	No		1955-05-22	1955-04-01	No
1951-11-29	1951-11-01	No		1955-06-20	1955-05-01	No
1951-12-28	1951-12-01	No		1955-07-19	1955-06-01	No
1952-01-27	1952-01-01	No		1955-08-18	1955-07-01	No
1952-02-25	1952-02-01	No		1955-09-16	1955-08-01	No
1952-03-26	1952-03-01	No		1955-10-16	1955-09-01	No
1952-04-24	1952-04-01	No		1955-11-14	1955-10-01	No
1952-05-24	1952-05-01	No		1955-12-14	1955-11-01	No
1952-06-22	1952-05-01	Yes		1956-01-13	1955-12-01	No
1952-07-22	1952-06-01	No		1956-02-12	1956-01-01	No
1952-08-20	1952-07-01	No		1956-03-12	1956-02-01	No
1952-09-19	1952-08-01	No		1956-04-11	1956-03-01	No
1952-10-19	1952-09-01	No		1956-05-10	1956-04-01	No
1952-11-17	1952-10-01	No		1956-06-09	1956-05-01	No
1952-12-17	1952-11-01	No		1956-07-08	1956-06-01	No
1953-01-15	1952-12-01	No		1956-08-06	1956-07-01	No
1953-02-14	1953-01-01	No		1956-09-05	1956-08-01	No
1953-03-15	1953-02-01	No		1956-10-04	1956-09-01	No
1953-04-14	1953-03-01	No		1956-11-03	1956-10-01	No
1953-05-13	1953-04-01	No		1956-12-02	1956-11-01	No
1953-06-11	1953-05-01	No		1957-01-01	1956-12-01	No
1953-07-11	1953-06-01	No		1957-01-31	1957-01-01	No
1953-08-10	1953-07-01	No		1957-03-02	1957-02-01	No

Date	Lunar	Leap Mth		Date	Lunar	Leap Mth
1957-03-31	1957-03-01	No		1960-10-20	1960-09-01	No
1957-04-30	1957-04-01	No		1960-11-19	1960-10-01	No
1957-05-29	1957-05-01	No		1960-12-18	1960-11-01	No
1957-06-28	1957-06-01	No		1961-01-17	1960-12-01	No
1957-07-27	1957-07-01	No		1961-02-15	1961-01-01	No
1957-08-25	1957-08-01	No		1961-03-17	1961-02-01	No
1957-09-24	1957-08-01	Yes		1961-04-15	1961-03-01	No
1957-10-23	1957-09-01	No		1961-05-15	1961-04-01	No
1957-11-22	1957-10-01	No		1961-06-13	1961-05-01	No
1957-12-21	1957-11-01	No		1961-07-13	1961-06-01	No
1958-01-20	1957-12-01	No		1961-08-11	1961-07-01	No
1958-02-18	1958-01-01	No		1961-09-10	1961-08-01	No
1958-03-20	1958-02-01	No		1961-10-10	1961-09-01	No
1958-04-19	1958-03-01	No		1961-11-08	1961-10-01	No
1958-05-19	1958-04-01	No		1961-12-08	1961-11-01	No
1958-06-17	1958 05 01	No		1962-01-06	1961-12-01	No
1958-07-17	1958-06-01	No		1962-02-05	1962-01-01	No
1958-08-15	1958-07-01	No		1962-03-06	1962-02-01	No
1958-09-13	1958-08-01	No		1962-04-05	1962-03-01	No
1958-10-13	1958-09-01	No		1962-05-04	1962-04-01	No
1958-11-11	1958-10-01	No		1962-06-02	1962-05-01	No
1958-12-11	1958-11-01	No		1962-07-02	1962-06-01	No
1959-01-09	1958-12-01	No		1962-07-31	1962-07-01	No
1959-02-08	1959-01-01	No		1962-08-30	1962-08-01	No
1959-03-09	1959-02-01	No		1962-09-29	1962-09-01	No
1959-04-08	1959-03-01	No		1962-10-28	1962-10-01	No
1959-05-08	1959-04-01	No		1962-11-27	1962-11-01	No
1959-06-06	1959-05-01	No		1962-12-27	1962-12-01	No
1959-07-06	1959-06-01	No		1963-01-25	1963-01-01	No
1959-08-04	1959-07-01	No		1963-02-24	1963-02-01	No
1959-09-03	1959-08-01	No		1963-03-25	1963-03-01	No
1959-10-02	1959-09-01	No		1963-04-24	1963-04-01	No
1959-11-01	1959-10-01	No		1963-05-23	1963-04-01	Yes
1959-11-30	1959-11-01	No		1963-06-21	1963-05-01	No
1959-12-30	1959-12-01	No		1963-07-21	1963-06-01	No
1960-01-28	1960-01-01	No		1963-08-19	1963-07-01	No
1960-02-27	1960-02-01	No		1963-09-18	1963-08-01	No
1960-03-27	1960-03-01	No		1963-10-17	1963-09-01	No
1960-04-26	1960-04-01	No		1963-11-16	1963-10-01	No
1960-05-25	1960-05-01	No		1963-12-16	1963-11-01	No
1960-06-24	1960-06-01	No		1964-01-15	1963-12-01	No
1960-07-24	1960-06-01	Yes		1964-02-13	1964-01-01	No
1960-08-22	1960-07-01	No		1964-03-14	1964-02-01	No
1960-09-21	1960-08-01	No		1964-04-12	1964-03-01	No

Date	Lunar	Leap Mth		Date	Lunar	Leap Mth
1964-05-12	1964-04-01	No		1967-12-02	1967-11-01	No
1964-06-10	1964-05-01	No		1967-12-31	1967-12-01	No
1964-07-09	1964-06-01	No		1968-01-30	1968-01-01	No
1964-08-08	1964-07-01	No		1968-02-28	1968-02-01	No
1964-09-06	1964-08-01	No		1968-03-29	1968-03-01	No
1964-10-06	1964-09-01	No		1968-04-27	1968-04-01	No
1964-11-04	1964-10-01	No		1968-05-27	1968-05-01	No
1964-12-04	1964-11-01	No		1968-06-26	1968-06-01	No
1965-01-03	1964-12-01	No		1968-07-25	1968-07-01	No
1965-02-02	1965-01-01	No		1968-08-24	1968-07-01	Yes
1965-03-03	1965-02-01	No		1968-09-22	1968-08-01	No
1965-04-02	1965-03-01	No		1968-10-22	1968-09-01	No
1965-05-01	1965-04-01	No		1968-11-20	1968-10-01	No
1965-05-31	1965-05-01	No		1968-12-20	1968-11-01	No
1965-06-29	1965-06-01	No		1969-01-18	1968-12-01	No
1965-07-28	1965-07-01	No		1969-02-17	1969-01-01	No
1965-08-27	1965-08-01	No		1969-03-18	1969-02-01	No
1965-09-25	1965-09-01	No		1969-04-17	1969-03-01	No
1965-10-24	1965-10-01	No		1969-05-16	1969-04-01	No
1965-11-23	1965-11-01	No		1969-06-15	1969-05-01	No
1965-12-23	1965-12-01	No		1969-07-14	1969-06-01	No
1966-01-21	1966-01-01	No		1969-08-13	1969-07-01	No
1966-02-20	1966-02-01	No		1969-09-12	1969-08-01	No
1966-03-22	1966-03-01	No		1969-10-11	1969-09-01	No
1966-04-21	1966-03-01	Yes		1969-11-10	1969-10-01	No
1966-05-20	1966-04-01	No		1969-12-09	1969-11-01	No
1966-06-19	1966-05-01	No		1970-01-08	1969-12-01	No
1966-07-18	1966-06-01	No		1970-02-06	1970-01-01	No
1966-08-16	1966-07-01	No		1970-03-08	1970-02-01	No
1966-09-15	1966-08-01	No		1970-04-06	1970-03-01	No
1966-10-14	1966-09-01	No		1970-05-05	1970-04-01	No
1966-11-12	1966-10-01	No		1970-06-04	1970-05-01	No
1966-12-12	1966-11-01	No		1970-07-03	1970-06-01	No
1967-01-11	1966-12-01	No		1970-08-02	1970-07-01	No
1967-02-09	1967-01-01	No		1970-09-01	1970-08-01	No
1967-03-11	1967-02-01	No		1970-09-30	1970-09-01	No
1967-04-10	1967-03-01	No		1970-10-30	1970-10-01	No
1967-05-09	1967-04-01	No		1970-11-29	1970-11-01	No
1967-06-08	1967-05-01	No		1970-12-28	1970-12-01	No
1967-07-08	1967-06-01	No		1971-01-27	1971-01-01	No
1967-08-06	1967-07-01	No		1971-02-25	1971-02-01	No
1967-09-04	1967-08-01	No		1971-03-27	1971-03-01	No
1967-10-04	1967-09-01	No		1971-04-25	1971-04-01	No
1967-11-02	1967-10-01	No		1971-05-24	1971-05-01	No

Date	Lunar	Leap Mth		Date	Lunar	Leap Mth
1971-06-23	1971-05-01	Yes		1975-01-12	1974-12-01	No
1971-07-22	1971-06-01	No		1975-02-11	1975-01-01	No
1971-08-21	1971-07-01	No		1975-03-13	1975-02-01	No
1971-09-19	1971-08-01	No		1975-04-12	1975-03-01	No
1971-10-19	1971-09-01	No		1975-05-11	1975-04-01	No
1971-11-18	1971-10-01	No		1975-06-10	1975-05-01	No
1971-12-18	1971-11-01	No		1975-07-09	1975-06-01	No
1972-01-16	1971-12-01	No		1975-08-07	1975-07-01	No
1972-02-15	1972-01-01	No		1975-09-06	1975-08-01	No
1972-03-15	1972-02-01	No		1975-10-05	1975-09-01	No
1972-04-14	1972-03-01	No		1975-11-03	1975-10-01	No
1972-05-13	1972-04-01	No		1975-12-03	1975-11-01	No
1972-06-11	1972-05-01	No		1976-01-01	1975-12-01	No
1972-07-11	1972-06-01	No		1976-01-31	1976-01-01	No
1972-08-09	1972-07-01	No		1976-03-01	1976-02-01	No
1972-09-08	1972-08-01	No		1976-03-31	1976-03-01	No
1972-10-07	1972-09-01	No		1976-04-29	1976-04-01	No
1972-11-06	1972-10-01	No		1976-05-29	1976-05-01	No
1972-12-06	1972-11-01	No		1976-06-27	1976-06-01	No
1973-01-04	1972-12-01	No		1976-07-27	1976-07-01	No
1973-02-03	1973-01-01	No		1976-08-25	1976-08-01	No
1973-03-05	1973-02-01	No		1976-09-24	1976-08-01	Yes
1973-04-03	1973-03-01	No		1976-10-23	1976-09-01	No
1973-05-03	1973-04-01	No		1976-11-21	1976-10-01	No
1973-06-01	1973-05-01	No		1976-12-21	1976-11-01	No
1973-06-30	1973-06-01	No		1977-01-19	1976-12-01	No
1973-07-30	1973-07-01	No		1977-02-18	1977-01-01	No
1973-08-28	1973-08-01	No		1977-03-20	1977-02-01	No
1973-09-26	1973-09-01	No		1977-04-18	1977-03-01	No
1973-10-26	1973-10-01	No		1977-05-18	1977-04-01	No
1973-11-25	1973-11-01	No		1977-06-17	1977-05-01	No
1973-12-24	1973-12-01	No		1977-07-16	1977-06-01	No
1974-01-23	1974-01-01	No		1977-08-15	1977-07-01	No
1974-02-22	1974-02-01	No		1977-09-13	1977-08-01	No
1974-03-24	1974-03-01	No		1977-10-13	1977-09-01	No
1974-04-22	1974-04-01	No		1977-11-11	1977-10-01	No
1974-05-22	1974-04-01	Yes		1977-12-11	1977-11-01	No
1974-06-20	1974-05-01	No		1978-01-09	1977-12-01	No
1974-07-19	1974-06-01	No		1978-02-07	1978-01-01	No
1974-08-18	1974-07-01	No		1978-03-09	1978-02-01	No
1974-09-16	1974-08-01	No		1978-04-07	1978-03-01	No
1974-10-15	1974-09-01	No		1978-05-07	1978-04-01	No
1974-11-14	1974-10-01	Yes		1978-06-06	1978-05-01	No
1974-12-14	1974-11-01	No		1978-07-05	1978-06-01	No

Date	Lunar	Leap Mth		Date	Lunar	Leap Mth
1978-08-04	1978-07-01	No		1982-02-24	1982-02-01	No
1978-09-03	1978-08-01	No		1982-03-25	1982-03-01	No
1978-10-02	1978-09-01	No		1982-04-24	1982-04-01	No
1978-11-01	1978-10-01	No		1982-05-23	1982-04-01	Yes
1978-11-30	1978-11-01	No		1982-06-21	1982-05-01	No
1978-12-30	1978-12-01	No		1982-07-21	1982-06-01	No
1979-01-28	1979-01-01	No		1982-08-19	1982-07-01	No
1979-02-27	1979-02-01	No		1982-09-17	1982-08-01	No
1979-03-28	1979-03-01	No		1982-10-17	1982-09-01	No
1979-04-26	1979-04-01	No		1982-11-15	1982-10-01	No
1979-05-26	1979-05-01	No		1982-12-15	1982-11-01	No
1979-06-24	1979-06-01	No		1983-01-14	1982-12-01	No
1979-07-24	1979-06-01	Yes		1983-02-13	1983-01-01	No
1979-08-23	1979-07-01	No		1983-03-15	1983-02-01	No
1979-09-21	1979-08-01	No		1983-04-13	1983-03-01	No
1979-10-21	1979-09-01	No		1983-05-13	1983-04-01	No
1979-11-20	1979-10-01	No		1983-06-11	1983-05-01	No
1979-12-19	1979-11-01	No		1983-07-10	1983-06-01	No
1980-01-18	1979-12-01	No		1983-08-09	1983-07-01	No
1980-02-16	1980-01-01	No		1983-09-07	1983-08-01	No
1980-03-17	1980-02-01	No		1983-10-06	1983-09-01	No
1980-04-15	1980-03-01	No		1983-11-05	1983-10-01	No
1980-05-14	1980-04-01	No		1983-12-04	1983-11-01	No
1980-06-13	1980-05-01	No		1984-01-03	1983-12-01	No
1980-07-12	1980-06-01	No		1984-02-02	1984-01-01	No
1980-08-11	1980-07-01	No		1984-03-03	1984-02-01	No
1980-09-09	1980-08-01	No		1984-04-01	1984-03-01	No
1980-10-09	1980-09-01	No		1984-05-01	1984-04-01	No
1980-11-08	1980-10-01	No		1984-05-31	1984-05-01	No
1980-12-07	1980-11-01	No		1984-06-29	1984-06-01	No
1981-01-06	1980-12-01	No		1984-07-28	1984-07-01	No
1981-02-05	1981-01-01	No		1984-08-27	1984-08-01	No
1981-03-06	1981-02-01	No		1984-09-25	1984-09-01	No
1981-04-05	1981-03-01	No		1984-10-24	1984-10-01	No
1981-05-04	1981-04-01	No		1984-11-23	1984-10-01	Yes
1981-06-02	1981-05-01	No		1984-12-22	1984-11-01	No
1981-07-02	1981-06-01	No		1985-01-21	1984-12-01	No
1981-07-31	1981-07-01	No		1985-02-20	1985-01-01	No
1981-08-29	1981-08-01	No		1985-03-21	1985-02-01	No
1981-09-28	1981-09-01	No		1985-04-20	1985-03-01	No
1981-10-28	1981-10-01	No		1985-05-20	1985-04-01	No
1981-11-26	1981-11-01	No		1985-06-18	1985-05-01	No
1981-12-26	1981-12-01	No		1985-07-18	1985-06-01	No
1982-01-25	1982-01-01	No		1985-08-16	1985-07-01	No

Date	Lunar	Leap Mth		Date	Lunar	Leap Mth
1985-09-15	1985-08-01	No		1989-04-06	1989-03-01	No
1985-10-14	1985-09-01	No		1989-05-05	1989-04-01	No
1985-11-12	1985-10-01	No		1989-06-04	1989-05-01	No
1985-12-12	1985-11-01	No		1989-07-03	1989-06-01	No
1986-01-10	1985-12-01	No		1989-08-02	1989-07-01	No
1986-02-09	1986-01-01	No		1989-08-31	1989-08-01	No
1986-03-10	1986-02-01	No		1989-09-30	1989-09-01	No
1986-04-09	1986-03-01	No		1989-10-29	1989-10-01	No
1986-05-09	1986-04-01	No		1989-11-28	1989-11-01	No
1986-06-07	1986-05-01	No		1989-12-28	1989-12-01	No
1986-07-07	1986-06-01	No		1990-01-27	1990-01-01	No
1986-08-06	1986-07-01	No		1990-02-25	1990-02-01	No
1986-09-04	1986-08-01	No		1990-03-27	1990-03-01	No
1986-10-04	1986-09-01	No		1990-04-25	1990-04-01	No
1986-11-02	1986-10-01	No		1990-05-24	1990-05-01	No
1986-12-02	1986-11-01	No		1990-06-23	1990-05-01	Yes
1986-12-31	1986-12-01	No		1990-07-22	1990-06-01	No
1987-01-29	1987-01-01	No		1990-08-20	1990-07-01	No
1987-02-28	1987-02-01	No		1990-09-19	1990-08-01	No
1987-03-29	1987-03-01	No		1990-10-18	1990-09-01	No
1987-04-28	1987-04-01	No		1990-11-17	1990-10-01	No
1987-05-27	1987-05-01	No		1990-12-17	1990-11-01	No
1987-06-26	1987-06-01	No		1991-01-16	1990-12-01	No
1987-07-26	1987-06-01	Yes		1991-02-15	1991-01-01	No
1987-08-24	1987-07-01	No		1991-03-16	1991-02-01	No
1987-09-23	1987-08-01	No		1991-04-15	1991-03-01	No
1987-10-23	1987-09-01	No		1991-05-14	1991-04-01	No
1987-11-21	1987-10-01	No		1991-06-12	1991-05-01	No
1987-12-21	1987-11-01	No		1991-07-12	1991-06-01	No
1988-01-19	1987-12-01	No		1991-08-10	1991-07-01	No
1988-02-17	1988-01-01	No		1991-09-08	1991-08-01	No
1988-03-18	1988-02-01	No		1991-10-08	1991-09-01	No
1988-04-16	1988-03-01	No		1991-11-06	1991-10-01	No
1988-05-16	1988-04-01	No		1991-12-06	1991-11-01	No
1988-06-14	1988-05-01	No		1992-01-05	1991-12-01	No
1988-07-14	1988-06-01	No		1992-02-04	1992-01-01	No
1988-08-12	1988-07-01	No		1992-03-04	1992-02-01	No
1988-09-11	1988-08-01	No		1992-04-03	1992-03-01	No
1988-10-11	1988-09-01	No		1992-05-03	1992-04-01	No
1988-11-09	1988-10-01	No		1992-06-01	1992-05-01	No
1988-12-09	1988-11-01	No		1992-06-30	1992-06-01	No
1989-01-08	1988-12-01	No		1992-07-30	1992-07-01	No
1989-02-06	1989-01-01	No		1992-08-28	1992-08-01	No
1989-03-08	1989-02-01	No		1992-09-26	1992-09-01	No

Date	Lunar	Leap Mth		Date	Lunar	Leap Mth
1992-10-26	1992-10-01	No		1996-05-17	1996-04-01	No
1992-11-24	1992-11-01	No		1996-06-16	1996-05-01	No
1992-12-24	1992-12-01	No		1996-07-16	1996-06-01	No
1993-01-23	1993-01-01	No		1996-08-14	1996-07-01	No
1993-02-21	1993-02-01	No		1996-09-13	1996-08-01	No
1993-03-23	1993-03-01	No		1996-10-12	1996-09-01	No
1993-04-22	1993-03-01	Yes		1996-11-11	1996-10-01	No
1993-05-21	1993-04-01	No		1996-12-11	1996-11-01	No
1993-06-20	1993-05-01	No		1997-01-09	1996-12-01	No
1993-07-19	1993-06-01	No		1997-02-07	1997-01-01	No
1993-08-18	1993-07-01	No		1997-03-09	1997-02-01	No
1993-09-16	1993-08-01	No		1997-04-07	1997-03-01	No
1993-10-15	1993-09-01	No		1997-05-07	1997-04-01	No
1993-11-14	1993-10-01	No		1997-06-05	1997-05-01	No
1993-12-13	1993-11-01	No		1997-07-05	1997-06-01	No
1994-01-12	1993-12-01	No		1997-08-03	1997-07-01	No
1994-02-10	1994-01-01	No		1997-09-02	1997-08-01	No
1994-03-12	1994-02-01	No		1997-10-02	1997-09-01	No
1994-04-11	1994-03-01	No		1997-10-31	1997-10-01	No
1994-05-11	1994-04-01	No		1997-11-30	1997-11-01	No
1994-06-09	1994-05-01	No		1997-12-30	1997-12-01	No
1994-07-09	1994-06-01	No		1998-01-28	1998-01-01	No
1994-08-07	1994-07-01	No		1998-02-27	1998-02-01	No
1994-09-06	1994-08-01	No		1998-03-28	1998-03-01	No
1994-10-05	1994-09-01	No		1998-04-26	1998-04-01	No
1994-11-03	1994-10-01	No		1998-05-26	1998-05-01	No
1994-12-03	1994-11-01	No		1998-06-24	1998-05-01	Yes
1995-01-01	1994-12-01	No		1998-07-23	1998-06-01	No
1995-01-31	1995-01-01	No		1998-08-22	1998-07-01	No
1995-03-01	1995-02-01	No		1998-09-21	1998-08-01	No
1995-03-31	1995-03-01	No		1998-10-20	1998-09-01	No
1995-04-30	1995-04-01	No		1998-11-19	1998-10-01	No
1995-05-29	1995-05-01	No		1998-12-19	1998-11-01	No
1995-06-28	1995-06-01	No		1999-01-17	1998-12-01	No
1995-07-27	1995-07-01	No		1999-02-16	1999-01-01	No
1995-08-26	1995-08-01	No		1999-03-18	1999-02-01	No
1995-09-25	1995-08-01	Yes		1999-04-16	1999-03-01	No
1995-10-24	1995-09-01	No		1999-05-15	1999-04-01	No
1995-11-22	1995-10-01	No		1999-06-14	1999-05-01	No
1995-12-22	1995-11-01	No		1999-07-13	1999-06-01	No
1996-01-20	1995-12-01	No		1999-08-11	1999-07-01	No
1996-02-19	1996-01-01	No		1999-09-10	1999-08-01	No
1996-03-19	1996-02-01	No		1999-10-09	1999-09-01	No
1996-04-18	1996-03-01	No		1999-11-08	1999-10-01	No

Date	Lunar	Leap Mth		Date	Lunar	Leap Mth
1999-12-08	1999-11-01	No		2003-06-30	2003-06-01	No
2000-01-07	1999-12-01	No		2003-07-29	2003-07-01	No
2000-02-05	2000-01-01	No		2003-08-28	2003-08-01	No
2000-03-06	2000-02-01	No		2003-09-26	2003-09-01	No
2000-04-05	2000-03-01	No		2003-10-25	2003-10-01	No
2000-05-04	2000-04-01	No		2003-11-24	2003-11-01	No
2000-06-02	2000-05-01	No		2003-12-23	2003-12-01	No
2000-07-02	2000-06-01	No		2004-01-22	2004-01-01	No
2000-07-31	2000-07-01	No		2004-02-20	2004-02-01	No
2000-08-29	2000-08-01	No		2004-03-21	2004-02-01	Yes
2000-09-28	2000-09-01	No		2004-04-19	2004-03-01	No
2000-10-27	2000-10-01	No		2004-05-19	2004-04-01	No
2000-11-26	2000-11-01	No		2004-06-18	2004-05-01	No
2000-12-26	2000-12-01	No		2004-07-17	2004-06-01	No
2001-01-24	2001-01-01	No		2004-08-16	2004-07-01	No
2001-02-23	2001-02-01	No		2004-09-14	2004-08-01	No
2001-03-25	2001-03-01	No		2004-10-14	2004-09-01	No
2001-04-23	2001-04-01	No		2004-11-12	2004-10-01	No
2001-05-23	2001-04-01	Yes		2004-12-12	2004-11-01	No
2001-06-21	2001-05-01	No		2005-01-10	2004-12-01	No
2001-07-21	2001-06-01	No		2005-02-09	2005-01-01	No
2001-08-19	2001-07-01	No		2005-03-10	2005-02-01	No
2001-09-17	2001-08-01	No		2005-04-09	2005-03-01	No
2001-10-17	2001-09-01	No		2005-05-08	2005-04-01	No
2001-11-15	2001-10-01	No		2005-06-07	2005-05-01	No
2001-12-15	2001-11-01	No		2005-07-06	2005-06-01	No
2002-01-13	2001-12-01	No		2005-08-05	2005-07-01	No
2002-02-12	2002-01-01	No		2005-09-04	2005-08-01	No
2002-03-14	2002-02-01	No		2005-10-03	2005-09-01	No
2002-04-13	2002-03-01	No		2005-11-02	2005-10-01	No
2002-05-12	2002-04-01	No		2005-12-01	2005-11-01	No
2002-06-11	2002-05-01	No		2005-12-31	2005-12-01	No
2002-07-10	2002-06-01	No		2006-01-29	2006-01-01	No
2002-08-09	2002-07-01	No		2006-02-28	2006-02-01	No
2002-09-07	2002-08-01	No		2006-03-29	2006-03-01	No
2002-10-06	2002-09-01	No		2006-04-28	2006-04-01	No
2002-11-05	2002-10-01	No		2006-05-27	2006-05-01	No
2002-12-04	2002-11-01	No		2006-06-26	2006-06-01	No
2003-01-03	2002-12-01	No		2006-07-25	2006-07-01	No
2003-02-01	2003-01-01	No		2006-08-24	2006-07-01	Yes
2003-03-03	2003-02-01	No		2006-09-22	2006-08-01	No
2003-04-02	2003-03-01	No		2006-10-22	2006-09-01	No
2003-05-01	2003-04-01	No		2006-11-21	2006-10-01	No
2003-05-31	2003-05-01	No		2006-12-20	2006-11-01	No

Date	Lunar	Leap Mth		Date	Lunar	Leap Mth
2007-01-19	2006-12-01	No		2010-08-10	2010-07-01	No
2007-02-18	2007-01-01	No		2010-09-08	2010-08-01	No
2007-03-19	2007-02-01	No		2010-10-08	2010-09-01	No
2007-04-17	2007-03-01	No		2010-11-06	2010-10-01	No
2007-05-17	2007-04-01	No		2010-12-06	2010-11-01	No
2007-06-15	2007-05-01	No		2011-01-04	2010-12-01	No
2007-07-14	2007-06-01	No		2011-02-03	2011-01-01	No
2007-08-13	2007-07-01	No		2011-03-05	2011-02-01	No
2007-09-11	2007-08-01	No		2011-04-03	2011-03-01	No
2007-10-11	2007-09-01	No		2011-05-03	2011-04-01	No
2007-11-10	2007-10-01	No		2011-06-02	2011-05-01	No
2007-12-10	2007-11-01	No		2011-07-01	2011-06-01	No
2008-01-08	2007-12-01	No		2011-07-31	2011-07-01	No
2008-02-07	2008-01-01	No		2011-08-29	2011-08-01	No
2008-03-08	2008-02-01	No		2011-09-27	2011-09-01	No
2008-04-06	2008-03-01	No		2011-10-27	2011-10-01	No
2008-05-05	2008-04-01	No		2011-11-25	2011-11-01	No
2008-06-04	2008-05-01	No		2011-12-25	2011-12-01	No
2008-07-03	2008-06-01	No		2012-01-23	2012-01-01	No
2008-08-01	2008-07-01	No		2012-02-22	2012-02-01	No
2008-08-31	2008-08-01	No		2012-03-22	2012-03-01	No
2008-09-29	2008-09-01	No		2012-04-21	2012-04-01	No
2008-10-29	2008-10-01	No		2012-05-21	2012-04-01	Yes
2008-11-28	2008-11-01	No		2012-06-19	2012-05-01	No
2008-12-27	2008-12-01	No		2012-07-19	2012-06-01	No
2009-01-26	2009-01-01	No		2012-08-17	2012-07-01	No
2009-02-25	2009-02-01	No		2012-09-16	2012-08-01	No
2009-03-27	2009-03-01	No		2012-10-15	2012-09-01	No
2009-04-25	2009-04-01	No		2012-11-14	2012-10-01	No
2009-05-24	2009-05-01	No		2012-12-13	2012-11-01	No
2009-06-23	2009-05-01	Yes		2013-01-12	2012-12-01	No
2009-07-22	2009-06-01	No		2013-02-10	2013-01-01	No
2009-08-20	2009-07-01	No		2013-03-12	2013-02-01	No
2009-09-19	2009-08-01	No		2013-04-10	2013-03-01	No
2009-10-18	2009-09-01	No		2013-05-10	2013-04-01	No
2009-11-17	2009-10-01	No		2013-06-08	2013-05-01	No
2009-12-16	2009-11-01	No		2013-07-08	2013-06-01	No
2010-01-15	2009-12-01	No		2013-08-07	2013-07-01	No
2010-02-14	2010-01-01	No		2013-09-05	2013-08-01	No
2010-03-16	2010-02-01	No		2013-10-05	2013-09-01	No
2010-04-14	2010-03-01	No		2013-11-03	2013-10-01	No
2010-05-14	2010-04-01	No		2013-12-03	2013-11-01	No
2010-06-12	2010-05-01	No		2014-01-01	2013-12-01	No
2010-07-12	2010-06-01	No		2014-01-31	2014-01-01	No

Date	Lunar	Leap Mth		Date	Lunar	Leap Mth
2014-03-01	2014-02-01	No		2017-09-20	2017-08-01	No
2014-03-31	2014-03-01	No		2017-10-20	2017-09-01	No
2014-04-29	2014-04-01	No		2017-11-18	2017-10-01	No
2014-05-29	2014-05-01	No		2017-12-18	2017-11-01	No
2014-06-27	2014-06-01	No		2018-01-17	2017-12-01	No
2014-07-27	2014-07-01	No		2018-02-16	2018-01-01	No
2014-08-25	2014-08-01	No		2018-03-17	2018-02-01	No
2014-09-24	2014-09-01	No		2018-04-16	2018-03-01	No
2014-10-24	2014-09-01	Yes		2018-05-15	2018-04-01	No
2014-11-22	2014-10-01	No		2018-06-14	2018-05-01	No
2014-12-22	2014-11-01	No		2018-07-13	2018-06-01	No
2015-01-20	2014-12-01	No		2018-08-11	2018-07-01	No
2015-02-19	2015-01-01	No		2018-09-10	2018-08-01	No
2015-03-20	2015-02-01	No		2018-10-09	2018-09-01	No
2015-04-19	2015-03-01	No		2018-11-08	2018-10-01	No
2015-05-18	2015-04-01	No		2018-12-07	2018-11-01	No
2015-06-16	2015-05-01	No		2019-01-06	2018-12-01	No
2015-07-16	2015-06-01	No		2019-02-05	2019-01-01	No
2015-08-14	2015-07-01	No		2019-03-07	2019-02-01	No
2015-09-13	2015-08-01	No		2019-04-05	2019-03-01	No
2015-10-13	2015-09-01	No		2019-05-05	2019-04-01	No
2015-11-12	2015-10-01	No		2019-06-03	2019-05-01	No
2015-12-11	2015-11-01	No		2019-07-03	2019-06-01	No
2016-01-10	2015-12-01	No		2019-08-01	2019-07-01	No
2016-02-08	2016-01-01	No		2019-08-30	2019-08-01	No
2016-03-09	2016-02-01	No		2019-09-29	2019-09-01	No
2016-04-07	2016-03-01	No		2019-10-28	2019-10-01	No
2016-05-07	2016-04-01	No		2019-11-26	2019-11-01	No
2016-06-05	2016-05-01	No		2019-12-26	2019-12-01	No
2016-07-04	2016-06-01	No		2020-01-25	2020-01-01	No
2016-08-03	2016-07-01	No		2020-02-23	2020-02-01	No
2016-09-01	2016-08-01	No		2020-03-24	2020-03-01	No
2016-10-01	2016-09-01	No		2020-04-23	2020-04-01	No
2016-10-31	2016-10-01	No		2020-05-23	2020-04-01	Yes
2016-11-29	2016-11-01	No		2020-06-21	2020-05-01	No
2016-12-29	2016-12-01	No		2020-07-21	2020-06-01	No
2017-01-28	2017-01-01	No		2020-08-19	2020-07-01	No
2017-02-26	2017-02-01	No		2020-09-17	2020-08-01	No
2017-03-28	2017-03-01	No		2020-10-17	2020-09-01	No
2017-04-26	2017-04-01	No		2020-11-15	2020-10-01	No
2017-05-26	2017-05-01	No		2020-12-15	2020-11-01	No
2017-06-24	2017-06-01	No		2021-01-13	2020-12-01	No
2017-07-23	2017-06-01	Yes		2021-02-12	2021-01-01	No
2017-08-22	2017-07-01	No		2021-03-13	2021-02-01	No

Date	Lunar	Leap Mth		Date	Lunar	Leap Mth
2021-04-12	2021-03-01	No		2024-11-01	2024-10-01	No
2021-05-12	2021-04-01	No		2024-12-01	2024-11-01	No
2021-06-10	2021-05-01	No		2024-12-31	2024-12-01	No
2021-07-10	2021-06-01	No		2025-01-29	2025-01-01	No
2021-08-08	2021-07-01	No		2025-02-28	2025-02-01	No
2021-09-07	2021-08-01	No		2025-03-29	2025-03-01	No
2021-10-06	2021-09-01	No		2025-04-28	2025-04-01	No
2021-11-05	2021-10-01	No		2025-05-27	2025-05-01	No
2021-12-04	2021-11-01	No		2025-06-25	2025-06-01	No
2022-01-03	2021-12-01	No		2025-07-25	2025-06-01	Yes
2022-02-01	2022-01-01	No		2025-08-23	2025-07-01	No
2022-03-03	2022-02-01	No		2025-09-22	2025-08-01	No
2022-04-01	2022-03-01	No		2025-10-21	2025-09-01	No
2022-05-01	2022-04-01	No		2025-11-20	2025-10-01	No
2022-05-30	2022-05-01	No		2025-12-20	2025-11-01	No
2022-06-29	2022-06-01	No		2026-01-19	2025-12-01	No
2022-07-29	2022-07-01	No		2026-02-17	2026-01-01	No
2022-08-27	2022-08-01	No		2026-03-19	2026-02-01	No
2022-09-26	2022-09-01	No		2026-04-17	2026-03-01	No
2022-10-25	2022-10-01	No		2026-05-17	2026-04-01	No
2022-11-24	2022-11-01	No		2026-06-15	2026-05-01	No
2022-12-23	2022-12-01	No		2026-07-14	2026-06-01	No
2023-01-22	2023-01-01	No		2026-08-13	2026-07-01	No
2023-02-20	2023-02-01	No		2026-09-11	2026-08-01	No
2023-03-22	2023-02-01	Yes		2026-10-10	2026-09-01	No
2023-04-20	2023-03-01	No		2026-11-09	2026-10-01	No
2023-05-19	2023-04-01	No		2026-12-09	2026-11-01	No
2023-06-18	2023-05-01	No		2027-01-08	2026-12-01	No
2023-07-18	2023-06-01	No		2027-02-06	2027-01-01	No
2023-08-16	2023-07-01	No		2027-03-08	2027-02-01	No
2023-09-15	2023-08-01	No		2027-04-07	2027-03-01	No
2023-10-15	2023-09-01	No		2027-05-06	2027-04-01	No
2023-11-13	2023-10-01	No		2027-06-05	2027-05-01	No
2023-12-13	2023-11-01	No		2027-07-04	2027-06-01	No
2024-01-11	2023-12-01	No		2027-08-02	2027-07-01	No
2024-02-10	2024-01-01	No		2027-09-01	2027-08-01	No
2024-03-10	2024-02-01	No		2027-09-30	2027-09-01	No
2024-04-09	2024-03-01	No		2027-10-29	2027-10-01	No
2024-05-08	2024-04-01	No		2027-11-28	2027-11-01	No
2024-06-06	2024-05-01	No		2027-12-28	2027-12-01	No
2024-07-06	2024-06-01	No		2028-01-26	2028-01-01	No
2024-08-04	2024-07-01	No		2028-02-25	2028-02-01	No
2024-09-03	2024-08-01	No		2028-03-26	2028-03-01	No
2024-10-03	2024-09-01	No		2028-04-25	2028-04-01	No

Date	Lunar	Leap Mth		Date	Lunar	Leap Mth
2028-05-24	2028-05-01	No		2029-10-08	2029-09-01	No
2028-06-23	2028-05-01	Yes		2029-11-06	2029-10-01	No
2028-07-22	2028-06-01	No		2029-12-05	2029-11-01	No
2028-08-20	2028-07-01	No		2030-01-04	2029-12-01	No
2028-09-19	2028-08-01	No		2030-02-03	2030-01-01	No
2028-10-18	2028-09-01	No		2030-03-04	2030-02-01	No
2028-11-16	2028-10-01	No		2030-04-03	2030-03-01	No
2028-12-16	2028-11-01	No		2030-05-02	2030-04-01	No
2029-01-15	2028-12-01	No		2030-06-01	2030-05-01	No
2029-02-13	2029-01-01	No		2030-07-01	2030-06-01	No
2029-03-15	2029-02-01	No		2030-07-30	2030-07-01	No
2029-04-14	2029-03-01	No		2030-08-29	2030-08-01	No
2029-05-13	2029-04-01	No		2030-09-27	2030-09-01	No
2029-06-12	2029-05-01	No		2030-10-27	2030-10-01	No
2029-07-11	2029-06-01	No		2030-11-25	2030-11-01	No
2029-08-10	2029-07-01	No		2030-12-25	2030-12-01	No
2029-09-08	2029-08-01	No				

How to use:

1. Based on your birth date, search the list above. For example, born 6th Feb 2011:

2011-01-04	2010-12-01	No
2011-02-03	2011-01-01	No
2011-03-05	2011-02-01	No

2. 6th Feb 2011 is between 3rd Feb 2011 and 5th Mar 2011. So, the entry: 3rd Feb 2011 is selected. 3rd Feb 2011 = 1st Day of 1st Lunar Month. So, 4th Feb = 2nd Day, 5th Feb = 3rd Day, 6th Feb = 4th Day.

3. Therefore, 6th Feb 2011 = 4th Day of 1st Lunar Month.

Index

237, 238, 239, 240, 252,
275, 276, 277, 278, 279,
281, 284, 285, 286, 287,
289, 290, 291, 292, 293,
294, 295, 296, 297, 298,
299, 300, 301, 302, 303,
304, 305, 306, 307, 309,
310, 311

He Tu, 39

Health, 92, 117, 118, 119, 120,
174, 202, 203, 204, 205,
206, 207, 208, 212, 213,
214, 215, 217, 218, 219,
220, 221, 222, 225, 226,
228, 230, 231, 232, 233,
234, 235, 236, 237, 238,
239, 240, 252, 275, 276,
277, 278, 279, 281, 284,
285, 286, 287, 289, 290,
291, 292, 293, 294, 295,
296, 297, 298, 299, 300,
301, 302, 303, 304, 305,
306, 307, 309, 310, 311

Heaven, Earth and Man, 46,
47, 48, 49

Heavenly Stems, 44, 51

Horse, 44

Hua Ji, 57, 63, 65, 67, 69, 73,
75, 85, 87, 88, 89, 147, 149,
150, 151, 153, 154, 155,
156, 157, 158, 159, 160,
161, 162, 163, 164, 165,
166, 167, 168, 169, 170,
171, 172, 173, 174, 175,
176, 177, 178, 179, 180,
181, 182, 183, 184, 185,
186, 187, 188, 189, 190,
191, 192, 193, 194, 195,
196, 197, 198, 199, 200,

204, 205, 211, 212, 215,
222, 229, 230, 231, 232,
233, 234, 235, 274, 278,
280, 281, 284, 285, 288,
289, 290, 291, 295, 301,
304, 307, 311

Hua Ke, 57, 61, 63, 73, 77, 87,
88, 89, 90, 91, 147, 150,
151, 152, 153, 154, 155,
156, 157, 158, 159, 160,
161, 162, 163, 164, 165,
166, 167, 168, 169, 170,
171, 172, 173, 174, 175,
176, 177, 178, 179, 180,
181, 182, 183, 184, 185,
186, 187, 188, 189, 190,
191, 192, 193, 194, 195, 196,
197, 198, 199, 200, 201,
211, 212, 225, 274, 278,
280, 281, 288, 291

Hua Lu, 57, 63, 65, 67, 69, 71,
73, 75, 77, 85, 87, 147, 148,
150, 151, 153, 154, 155,
156, 158, 159, 160, 162,
163, 164, 166, 167, 168,
170, 171, 172, 174, 175,
176, 178, 179, 180, 181,
182, 183, 184, 186, 187,
188, 190, 191, 192, 194,
195, 196, 198, 199, 200,
204, 210, 212, 221, 225,
231, 274, 278, 280, 281,
284, 288, 291, 292, 297,
298, 300, 301, 307, 311

Hua Quan, 57, 61, 63, 67, 69,
71, 73, 75, 77, 85, 87, 147,
148, 150, 151, 153, 154,
155, 156, 157, 158, 159,
160, 162, 163, 164, 166,

211, 212, 217, 218, 219,
220, 221, 222, 223, 224,
225, 228, 242, 243, 244,
255, 256, 257, 258, 259,
260, 261, 274, 275, 276,
277, 278, 279, 280, 281,
287, 289, 290, 291, 292,
293, 294, 295, 296, 297,
298, 299, 300, 301, 302,
303, 304, 305, 306, 307,
309, 310, 311
Taiji, 41, 42
Tan Lang, 59, 66, 67, 94, 99,
103, 108, 113, 117, 122,
125, 130, 134, 139, 142,
150, 151, 155, 158, 162,
166, 170, 174, 178, 182,
186, 190, 194, 198, 212,
214, 215, 217, 218, 219,
220, 221, 222, 223, 224,
225, 228, 241, 243, 244,
255, 256, 257, 258, 259,
260, 261,274, 275, 276, 277,
278, 279, 280, 281, 286,
287, 289, 290, 291, 292,
293, 294, 295, 296, 297,
298, 299, 300, 301, 302,
303, 304, 305, 306, 307,
309, 310, 311
Tian Fu, 59, 80, 81, 96, 100,
104, 109, 114, 119, 123,
127, 131, 136, 140, 144,
151, 212, 217, 218, 219,
220, 221, 222, 223, 224,
225, 228, 241, 243, 244,
255, 256, 257, 258, 259,
260, 261, 275, 276, 277,
278, 279, 281, 287, 289,
290, 291, 292, 293, 294,

295, 296, 297, 298, 299,
300, 301, 302, 303, 304,
305, 306, 307, 309, 310, 311
Tian Ji, 59, 72, 95, 99, 103,
108, 113, 118, 122, 126,
130, 135, 139, 143, 150,
151, 153, 155, 159, 163,
167, 171, 175, 179, 183,
187, 191, 195, 199, 212,
217, 218, 219, 220, 221,
222, 223, 224, 225, 228,
241, 242, 255, 256, 257,
258, 259, 260, 261, 274,
275, 276, 277, 278, 279,
280, 281, 287, 288, 289,
290, 291, 292, 293, 294,
295, 296, 297, 298, 299,
300, 301, 302, 303, 304,
305, 306, 307, 309, 310, 311
Tian Liang, 59, 76, 95, 100,
104, 109, 114, 118, 123,
126, 131, 135, 139, 143,
150, 151, 153, 156, 159,
164, 168, 171, 176, 180,
184, 188, 191, 196, 199,
212, 217, 218, 219, 220,
221, 222, 223, 224, 225,
228, 242, 255, 256, 257,
258, 259, 260, 261, 274,
275, 276, 277, 278, 280,
281, 287, 289, 290, 291,
292, 293, 294, 295, 296,
297, 298, 299, 300, 301,
302, 303, 304, 305, 306,
307, 309, 310, 311
Tian Tong, 59, 74, 95, 99, 104,
109, 114, 118, 122, 126,
131, 135, 139, 143, 150,
151, 156, 159, 163, 167,

171, 175, 180, 183, 188, 191, 195, 199, 212, 217, 218, 219, 220, 221, 222, 223, 224, 225, 228, 243, 244, 255, 256, 257, 258, 259, 260, 261, 274, 275, 276, 277, 278, 279, 280, 281, 287, 288, 289, 290, 291, 292, 293, 294, 295, 296, 297, 298, 299, 300, 301, 302, 303, 304, 305, 306, 307, 309, 310, 311

Tian Xiang, 59, 82, 96, 100, 104, 109, 114, 119, 123, 127, 131, 136, 140, 144, 151, 212, 217, 218, 219, 220, 221, 222, 223, 224, 225, 228, 241, 244, 255, 256, 257, 258, 259, 260, 261, 275, 276, 277, 278, 281, 287, 288, 289, 290, 291, 292, 293, 294, 295, 296, 297, 298, 299, 300, 301, 302, 303, 304, 305, 306, 307, 309, 310, 311

Travel, 92, 121, 122, 123, 124, 178, 202, 203, 204, 205, 206, 207, 208, 212, 213, 214, 215, 217, 218, 219, 220, 221, 222, 225, 226, 227, 228, 230, 231, 232, 233, 234, 235, 236, 237, 238, 239, 240, 252, 275, 276, 277, 278, 279, 281, 284, 285, 286, 287, 289, 290, 291, 292, 293, 294, 295, 296, 297, 298, 299, 300, 301, 302, 303, 304, 305, 306, 307, 309, 310, 311

Water, 39, 42, 43, 44, 45, 59, 66, 68, 70, 74, 82, 86, 89, 91, 149, 151, 253, 274, 309, 310, 311

Wealth, 62, 68, 80, 86, 92, 112, 113, 114, 115, 116, 170, 202, 203, 204, 205, 206, 207, 208, 210, 212, 213, 214, 217, 218, 219, 220, 221, 222, 225, 226, 227, 228, 230, 231, 232, 234, 235, 236, 237, 238, 239, 240, 252, 275, 276, 277, 278, 279, 281, 283, 284, 285, 286, 287, 288, 289, 290, 291, 292, 293, 294, 295, 296, 297, 298, 299, 300, 301, 302, 303, 304, 305, 306, 307, 309, 310, 311

Wen Chang, 59, 88, 89, 97, 101, 105, 110, 115, 119, 124, 128, 132, 137, 141, 144, 150, 151, 155, 157, 160, 165, 168, 172, 177, 181, 184, 189, 192, 196, 200, 212, 221, 226, 242, 244, 246, 267, 268, 269, 270, 271, 272, 273, 274, 275, 276, 277, 278, 279, 280, 281, 287, 288, 289, 290, 291, 292, 293, 294, 295, 296, 297, 298, 299, 300, 301, 302, 303, 304, 305, 306, 307, 309, 310, 311

Wen Qu, 59, 89, 97, 101, 106, 110, 115, 119, 124, 128, 132, 137, 141, 145, 150, 151, 155, 157, 160, 165, 168, 173, 177, 181, 185,

189, 192, 197, 200, 212,
226, 242, 244, 246, 267,
268, 269, 270, 271, 272,
273, 274, 275, 276, 277,
278, 279, 280, 281, 287,
289, 290, 291, 292, 293,
294, 295, 296, 297, 298,
299, 300, 301, 302, 303,
304, 305, 306, 307, 309,
310, 311
West, 148
Wife, 86, 102
Winter, 44, 51, 149
Winter Solstice, 51
Wood, 39, 40, 42, 43, 44, 45,
59, 66, 72, 147, 151, 253,
274, 296, 297, 298, 299,
300, 301, 302
Wu Qu, 59, 62, 93, 98, 102,
107, 112, 117, 121, 125,
129, 134, 138, 142, 150,
151, 154, 158, 162, 166,
170, 174, 178, 182, 186,
190, 194, 198, 212, 217,
218, 219, 220, 221, 222,
223, 224, 225, 228, 243,
255, 256, 257, 258, 259,
260, 261, 274, 275, 276,
277, 278, 279, 280, 281,
283, 287, 288, 289, 290,
291, 292, 293, 294, 295,
296, 297, 298, 299, 300,
301, 302, 303, 304, 305,
306, 307, 309, 310, 311
Yearly, 202, 246, 277
You Bi, 59, 91, 97, 101, 106,
111, 116, 120, 124, 128,
133, 137, 141, 145, 150,
151, 154, 157, 161, 165,

169, 173, 177, 181, 185,
189, 193, 197, 201, 212,
227, 246, 261, 262, 263,
264, 265, 266, 267, 274,
275, 276, 277, 278, 279,
280, 281, 287, 289, 290,
291, 292, 293, 294, 295,
296, 297, 298, 299, 300,
301, 302, 303, 304, 305,
306, 307, 309, 310, 311
Zi Wei, 1, 3, 33, 36, 37, 38,
50, 56, 57, 58, 59, 60, 80,
92, 93, 98, 102, 107, 112,
117, 121, 125, 129, 134,
138, 142, 146, 150, 151,
152, 153, 154, 158, 162,
166, 170, 174, 178, 182,
186, 190, 194, 198, 202,
212, 216, 217, 218, 219,
220, 221, 222, 223, 224,
225, 228, 236, 241, 246,
254, 255, 256, 257, 258,
259, 260, 261, 274, 275,
276, 277, 278, 279, 280,
281, 282, 283, 284, 287,
289, 290, 291, 292, 293,
294, 295, 296, 297, 298,
299, 300, 301, 302, 303,
304, 305, 306, 307, 309,
310, 311
Zi Wei Dou Shu, 1, 33, 36, 37,
38, 50, 56, 57, 58, 59, 92,
146, 150, 152, 202, 212,
216, 236, 246, 282, 283,
284, 287, 305
Zuo Fu, 59, 90, 97, 101, 106,
110, 115, 120, 124, 128,
133, 137, 141, 145, 150,
151, 154, 157, 161, 165,

169, 173, 177, 181, 185,
189, 193, 197, 200, 212,
227, 246, 261, 262, 263,
264, 265, 266, 267, 274,
275, 276, 277, 278, 279,

280, 281, 287, 288, 289,
290, 291, 292, 293, 294,
295, 296, 297, 298, 299,
300, 301, 302, 303, 304,
305, 306, 307, 309, 310, 311